California in the 60s.

Benjamin's got excellent grades, very proud parents and, since he helped Mrs Robinson with her zipper, a fine future behind him . . .

A cult novel, a classic film, a quintessential hit of the 60s, now Benjamin's disastrous sexual odyssey is brought vividly to life in this world stage premiere production.

Terry Johnson's work as a playwright includes *Dead Funny*, which opened at the Hampstead Theatre and enjoyed two successful West End runs at the Vaudeville and Savoy Theatres, and *Hysteria*, last seen at the Duke of Yorks Theatre as part of the Royal Court Classics season. Also recently revived at the Donmar Warehouse was *Insignificance*. Earlier work includes *Amabel* and *Unsuitable for Adults* at The Bush, *Imagine Drowning* at Hampstead, and *Cries from the Mammal House* at the Royal Court. Work for the Royal National Theatre includes his adaptation of Edward Ravenscroft's *The London Cuckolds*, Philip Ridley's *Sparkleshark* and his own most recent play *Cleo, Camping, Emmanuelle and Dick*, which won the Olivier Award for Best Comedy. His work has been performed all over Great Britain, in major US cities, Australia, Europe, Israel, Ireland and Canada. He is the recipient of some major British theatre awards including Playwright of the Year 1995, Critics' Circle Best New Play 1995, Writers' Guild Best West End Play 1995, Olivier Award Best Comedy 1994, the Mayer-Whitworth Award 1993 and the John Whiting Award 1991. Recent work as a director includes Shelagh Stephenson's *The Memory of Water* (Vaudeville Theatre) and David Farr's *Elton John's Glasses* (Queen's Theatre). In 1996 he directed the American premiere of Stephen Jeffries' *The Libertine* for Steppenwolf Theatre in Chicago. For television he directed the film of *Neville's Island* by Tim Firth and contributed two dramas, *Blood and Water* and *The Chemistry Lesson*, to the BBC Ghosts season. Earlier television work includes the adaptation of Alan Ayckbourn's *Way Upstream* and Nick Dunning's *The Lorelei* for the BBC. He has recently finished the film of *Cleo, Camping, Emmanuelle and Dick*, cunningly re-titled *Cor, Blimey!*

Published by Methuen 2000

1 3 5 7 9 10 8 6 4 2

First published in the Great Britain in 2000 by Methuen Publishing Limited
215 Vauxhall Bridge Road, London SW1V 1EJ

Methuen Publishing Limited Reg. No. 3543167

A CIP catalogue record for this book is available from the British Library

ISBN 0 413 75400 6

Typeset by SX Composing DTP, Rayleigh, Essex
Printed and bound in Great Britain by
Cox & Wyman Ltd, Reading, Berkshire

The Graduate

a play by

Terry Johnson

based on the novel by Charles Webb *and the screenplay by* Calder Willingham *and* Buck Henry

Methuen

The Graduate was first presented by John Reid and Sacha
Brooks at the Gielgud Theatre, London, on 24 March 2000,
with the following cast (in order of appearance):

Benjamin Braddock   Matthew Rhys
Mr Braddock   Paul Jesson
Mr Robinson   Colin Stinton
Mr Braddock   Amanda Boxer
Mrs Robinson   Kathleen Turner
Elaine Robinson   Kelly Reilly

Desk Clerk, Waiter, Psychiatrist   Alan Barnes
Belligerent Man, Priest   Geoffrey Towers
Stripper   Sally Chattaway
Wedding Guests   Sara Bienvenu
                                 Josh Cohen

Director Terry Johnson
Set & Costume Designer Rob Howell
Lighting Designer Hugh Vanstone
Sound Designer Mike Walker
Music Barrington Pheloung & Original Artists
Assistant Director Caroline Hadley
Company Stage Manager Alan Hatton
Deputy Stage Manager Natalie Wood
Assistant Stage Managers Marcus Watson
                                Rosemary McIntosh

Produced by special arrangement with Canal+ Image
Executive for Canal+ Image Ron Halpern

Characters

Benjamin
Mrs Robinson
Mr Robinson
Elaine
Dad, Mr Braddock
Mom, Mrs Braddock
Stripper
Desk Clerk
Two Men
Psychiatrist
Wedding Guests
Priest

The Desk Clerk doubles the Priest and the Psychiatrist. The Two Men and the Wedding Guests are doubled by the company.

Setting

California, 1960's.

A flexible, minimalist setting with one door USR and another DSL. Simple furnishings transform the space into: Benjamin's bedroom; the lobby of the Taft Hotel; Room 515, the Taft Hotel; a downtown bar; the Robinsons' living room; the Braddocks' poolside; a rooming house bedroom, Berkeley; a vestry; a motel room.

The light beyond the windows of these rooms is bright and Californian, slamming through curtains or blinds, lending sharp contrast to the interiors. Similarly, the night scenes share the illusion of illumination from source, with rich amber light spilling from lamps or through doors, sculpting well-defined playing areas from deep shadow.

The effect should be slightly claustrophobic.

Act One

Scene One

In the darkness, the sound of amplified breathing as if through an oxygen mask.

Lights come up on **Benjamin***'s room. Door to en suite bathroom, door to hallway. A bed, a chair. Airfix aeroplanes. A fish-tank.*

It's night. **Benjamin** *sits in semi-darkness amidst the remnants of his pre-pubescence. He is perfectly still, and wears a diving suit. The sounds of a party filtering up from downstairs. The door opens to throw a shaft of bright light across the room.* **Benjamin***'s father silhouetted.*

Dad Ben? Ben?

Ben *removes the mask.*

Dad What are you doing?

Benjamin You said I should put the suit on.

Dad I said you should put the suit on and come downstairs.

Benjamin I put the suit on.

Dad Then come on downstairs.

Benjamin I lost the inclination.

Dad It's a hell of a suit, isn't it?

Benjamin Yes, it is.

Dad Happy graduation.

Benjamin Thank you.

Dad So, come on down.

Benjamin I'll be down.

Dad　The guests are all here.

Benjamin　I'll be down soon.

Dad　What is it, Ben?

Benjamin　Nothing.

Dad　Then why don't you come down and see your guests?

Benjamin　I have some things on my mind right now.

Dad　What things?

Benjamin　Just some things.

Dad　Ben, these are our friends down there. You owe them a little courtesy.

Benjamin　I'd rather be alone right now.

Dad　Hal Robinson and I have been doing business together in this town for seventeen years. He's the best friend I have. He has a client in Chicago that he's put off seeing so he could be here tonight . . .

Benjamin　I don't want to see the Robinsons.

Dad　The Terhunes have come all the way from . . .

Benjamin　I don't want to see the Terhunes. I don't want to see the Robinsons, the Terhunes, the Pearsons or anyone else.

Dad　I don't know what's got into you but whatever it is I want you to snap out of it and march right on down there!

Benjamin　I just need to be alone right now.

The door opens and **Mr Robinson** *strides in with* **Benjamin**'s *mother.*

Mr Robinson　All hail the conquering hero!

Mom　Ben, where are you?

Benjamin　I'm here.

Mr Robinson   Ben!

Benjamin   Mr Robinson.

Dad   He's wearing the suit.

Mom   You're wearing the suit!

Dad   He loves it.

Mom   Do you like it Ben?

Dad   He'd better, or I'm out a coupla hundred bucks!

Mr Robinson   It's a hell of a suit.

Dad   Isn't it?

Mom   Ben, the guests are all downstairs.

Dad   Come on Ben, let's go down.

Mr Robinson   Ben, I want to shake your hand. Goddammit I'm proud of you.

Mom   We're all so proud of you, Ben.

Dad   Everyone's lining up down there to shake your hand.

Mr Robinson   I took a look at your yearbook, Ben. Head of the debating club. Captain of cross-country. Editor of the school newspaper.

Dad   No one appears in that yearbook more than Ben.

Mr Robinson   Social secretary of his house. I'm running out of fingers . . . First in your class . . .

Benjamin   I wasn't first.

Mr Robinson   Oh?

Benjamin   I *tied* for first. I tied with Abe Frankel.

Mr Robinson   Well, the luck of the Jews. Now give me the low-down on that prize of yours.

Benjamin   Well, I'm not . . .

Dad   Tell him about it, Ben.

Mom   It's called the Frank Halpingham Education Award and it puts Ben through two years of graduate school when he goes into teaching.

Mr Robinson   And they chose Ben.

Dad   He's into Harvard and he's into Yale. And what's that other one?

Mom   Columbia.

Dad   Columbia.

Mr Robinson   Well . . . good God Frank, you bred a genius.

Dad   I guess we did.

Mom   I don't know how.

Dad   We don't know where he got it from, but well yes, Ben has quite an intellect.

Mr Robinson   I've got one thing to say to you Ben. May I say one thing to your son?

Dad   Go right ahead.

Mr Robinson   I've just got one thing to say, Ben.

Benjamin   What's that, sir?

Mr Robinson   One word, Ben.

Benjamin   One word?

Mr Robinson   Plastics, Ben. Plastics. Will you think about that?

Benjamin   Yes I will.

Mom   Benjamin is going to teach; aren't you Ben?

Benjamin   Well . . .

Dad   Don't hound the boy, now.

Mom   Well . . .

Dad   Whatever this boy does . . .

Mr Robinson   Whatever he chooses to do . . .

Dad   This boy is gonna shine.

Mr Robinson   I couldn't be prouder of you Ben, if you were my own son.

Dad (*touched*)   Thank you, Hal. Say thank you, Ben.

Benjamin   Thank you.

Mr Robinson   I have to get to the airport.

Dad   You need a cab?

Mr Robinson   I'm gonna drive. My wife will need a cab.

Dad   We'll put her in a cab.

Mr Robinson   Just wait until you can't stand her a moment longer, then put her in a cab. Call a cab and just pour her in.

Mom   Oh scoot.

Dad   She knows how to enjoy herself.

Mr Robinson   She certainly does.

Mom   She just needed a little lie down, that's all she needed.

Mr Robinson   Ben, don't be a stranger.

Mr Robinson *leaves*.

Dad (*turning*)   Ben, you come on down now. Are you coming down, Ben?

Benjamin   No I'm not.

Dad   Those people down there . . .

Benjamin   Those people down there are grotesque!

Dad   Grotesque?

Benjamin   And you're grotesque.

Dad   You're calling me grotesque?

Benjamin   You are grotesque, and *I'm* grotesque, we're all grotesque. Not actually grotesque, you're not grotesque, but I have this feeling of grotesqueness when I even think about leaving this room, all right?

Dad   Ben, you're all tied up in knots. You've just had the four most strenuous years of your life back there . . .

Benjamin   They were nothing.

Dad   Four golden years . . .

Benjamin   Which add up to nothing.

Dad   I'm going to have words with you later. I'm going downstairs to tell these people you are suddenly sick, and I am going to entertain these people on your behalf. And I do not wish to see your face.

Benjamin's *father leaves.*

Mom   Are you sick, Ben?

Benjamin   Oh, yes.

Mom   Well then I guess you'd better get out of that suit.

Benjamin's *mother leaves.* **Benjamin** *struggles to get out of the suit. The door opens to silhouette* **Mrs Robinson**. *She watches* **Benjamin** *as he struggles, half undressed.*

Mrs Robinson   I guess this isn't the spare room, is it?

Benjamin   Oh good God . . . evening, Mrs Robinson.

Mrs Robinson   Good evening, Benjamin.

Benjamin   It's down the hall.

Mrs Robinson   That's a hell of a thing.

Benjamin   Yes, it is. Would you excuse me?

He struggles to make himself decent. **Mrs Robinson** *watches.*

Mrs Robinson   Is this what they're wearing back east?

Benjamin   It's a graduation gift.

Mrs Robinson   You sleep in it?

Benjamin   My father wanted me to show it off. He wanted a demonstration in the pool.

Mrs Robinson   It looks like a prophylactic.

Benjamin   A what?

Mrs Robinson   For the severely anxious.

Benjamin   It's at the end of the hall.

Mrs Robinson   What is?

Benjamin   The spare room.

Mrs Robinson   Ah.

Mrs Robinson *enters the room, a little unsteady.*

Benjamin   Mrs Robinson, I'm kind of distraught at the moment. I'm sorry to be rude but I have some things on my mind. It's good to see you.

Mrs Robinson   How are you?

Benjamin   I'm sorry not to be more congenial, but I'm trying to think.

Mrs Robinson   Is there an ashtray in here?

Benjamin   No.

He meant she should leave. She lights a cigarette. He takes her the waste bin. She puts her match in it.

Mrs Robinson   What are you upset about?

Benjamin   Some personal things.

Mrs Robinson   Girl trouble?

Benjamin   What?

Mrs Robinson   Do you have girl trouble?

Benjamin   Look, I'm sorry to be this way but I'm just, well right now I'm sort of . . .

Mrs Robinson   I was feeling a little unsteady myself. Your mother said I should lie down for a while.

Benjamin   The spare room's at the end of the hall.

Mrs Robinson   Are you drinking?

Benjamin   I don't drink.

Mrs Robinson   You don't drink?

Benjamin   As a rule. Of course I drink, but not as a rule.

Mrs Robinson   What do you drink? Bourbon?

Benjamin   Mrs Robinson, I have some things on my mind. And I have guests downstairs I should . . .

Mrs Robinson   May I ask you a question?

Benjamin   Uh-huh.

Mrs Robinson   What do you think of me?

Benjamin   What?

Mrs Robinson   What do you think of me?

Benjamin   Um . . .

Mrs Robinson   You've known me nearly all your life, you must think something . . .

Benjamin   Look, this is a rather strange conversation and I really ought to get downstairs . . .

Mrs Robinson   Don't you have any opinions at all?

Benjamin   No. Look, my father may be up again any minute, and . . .

Mrs Robinson   Benjamin.

Benjamin   What?

Mrs Robinson   Did you know I was an alcoholic?

Benjamin   Mrs Robinson, I don't want to talk about this.

Mrs Robinson   Did you know that?

Benjamin   No.

Mrs Robinson   You never suspected?

Benjamin   No.

Mrs Robinson   My God Benjamin, I fall out of cars. I insult senators at fondue parties. Surely you must have formed some sort of . . .

Benjamin   Mrs Robinson, this is none of my business . . .

Mrs Robinson   You never even suspected?

Benjamin   Would you excuse me?

Mrs Robinson   Sit down.

Benjamin   I'm going downstairs now.

Mrs Robinson   Why?

Benjamin   Because I want to be alone.

Mrs Robinson   There are three dozen people down there.

Benjamin   Then I'll go for a walk. I need to get out of here.

Benjamin *puts on a raincoat. It's older than he is.*

Mrs Robinson   Would you drive me home?

Benjamin   I'm sorry?

Mrs Robinson   I want you to drive me home. My husband's flying to Chicago. I don't like to be alone.

Benjamin   My God.

Mrs Robinson   What?

Benjamin   No. No, Mrs Robinson. Oh no.

Mrs Robinson   What's wrong?

Benjamin   Mrs Robinson, you didn't – I mean you didn't expect . . .

Mrs Robinson   What?

Benjamin   I mean you didn't really think I would do something like that.

Mrs Robinson   Like what?

Benjamin   What do you think!

Mrs Robinson   Well, I don't know.

Benjamin   For God's sake Mrs Robinson, you come to my room, you sit on the bed, you . . . smoke a cigarette, then you start opening up your personal life to me and now you're asking me to take you home because your husband's flying to Chicago.

Mrs Robinson   So?

Benjamin   Mrs Robinson, you are trying to seduce me. (*Certain.*) Aren't you. (*Uncertain.*) Aren't you?

Mrs Robinson   Why no. I hadn't thought of it. I feel rather flattered that you . . .

Benjamin (*mortified*)   Mrs Robinson, would you forgive me?

Mrs Robinson   What?

Benjamin   Will you forgive me for what I just said?

Mrs Robinson   It's all right.

Benjamin   It's not all right. That's the worst thing I've ever said to anyone!

Mrs Robinson   I've heard worse.

Benjamin   Please forgive me. Because I don't think of you that way. It's just I'm all mixed up.

Mrs Robinson   All right, calm down.

Benjamin   It makes me sick that I said that to you.

Mrs Robinson   I forgive you.

Benjamin   Can you? Can you ever forget I said that?

Mrs Robinson   We'll forget it right now.

Benjamin   I don't know what's wrong with me.

Mrs Robinson   It's forgotten.

Benjamin   Good.

Mrs Robinson   Benjamin?

Benjamin   Yes?

She stands and turns her back to him.

Mrs Robinson   Would you unzip my dress?

Benjamin   Un your what?

Mrs Robinson   Your mother said I should lie down. The spare bed is piled high with coats. Do you mind if I lie down, Benjamin?

Benjamin   No. Be my guest. Good night.

Mrs Robinson   Benjamin, would you please unzip the dress?

Benjamin   I'd rather not.

Mrs Robinson   Do you still think I'm trying to seduce you?

Benjamin   No I don't.

Mrs Robinson   With your parents just downstairs?

Benjamin   I ought to go down . . .

Mrs Robinson   You've known me all your life.

Benjamin   I know that.

Mrs Robinson   Would you please? It's hard for me to reach.

After a moment, **Benjamin** *unzips her dress.*

Thank you.

Benjamin   You're welcome.

Mrs Robinson   What are you scared of?

Benjamin   I'm not scared of anything.

Mrs Robinson   Then why do you keep moving away?

Benjamin   Because this is my room and if you're going to lie down I don't think I should be here.

She lets her dress fall.

Mrs Robinson   Haven't you ever seen anyone in a slip before?

Benjamin   Not in my parents' house, no.

Mrs Robinson   You still think I'm trying to seduce you, don't you?

Benjamin   No. But what if they walked in?

Mrs Robinson   Well, what if they did?

Benjamin   Well it would look pretty funny, wouldn't it?

Mrs Robinson   Do you think they'd be horrified that you saw me in my slip?

Benjamin   Well, they might get the wrong idea.

Mrs Robinson   I don't see why. I'm twice your age.

Benjamin   That's not the point.

Mrs Robinson   Benjamin, I am not trying to seduce you!

Benjamin   I know that.

Mrs Robinson   Would you like me to seduce you?

Benjamin   What?

Mrs Robinson   Is that what you're trying to tell me?

Benjamin   I'm going downstairs now. I apologise for what I said. I hope you can forget about it. I'm going downstairs.

He steps out the door.

Mrs Robinson   Benjamin.

Benjamin   What?

Mrs Robinson   Could you bring me my purse before you go?

Benjamin   No.

Mrs Robinson   Please?

Benjamin   I have to go downstairs.

Mrs Robinson   I really don't want to put this on again; won't you bring it to me?

Benjamin   Where is it?

Mrs Robinson   In the spare room. Beside the bed.

Benjamin   I'll get your purse. Then I have to go downstairs.

He leaves. **Mrs Robinson** *finishes her drink and goes into the bathroom, leaving the door ajar.* **Benjamin** *returns.*

Mrs Robinson?

Mrs Robinson (*off*)   I'm in the bathroom.

Benjamin   Well, here's your purse.

Mrs Robinson (*off*)   Could you bring it in?

Benjamin   I'll hand it to you.

Mrs Robinson (*off*)   Benjamin, I'm getting pretty tired of this.

Benjamin   What?

Mrs Robinson (*off*)   I'm getting pretty tired of all this suspicion. Now if you won't do me a simple favour, then I don't know what.

Benjamin   I'll put it on the bed.

Mrs Robinson (*off*)   For God's sake Benjamin, will you hand me the goddam purse.

Benjamin   I'd rather not.

Mrs Robinson (*off*)   All right then, put it on the bed.

Benjamin   OK. It's on the bed.

He crosses the room to the bed. **Mrs Robinson** *crosses the room behind him, closes the door and turns the key. She is naked.*

Benjamin   Oh, God.

She looks at him.

Oh, my God.

Mrs Robinson   Don't be nervous.

Benjamin   Let me out.

Mrs Robinson   Benjamin?

Benjamin   Get away from that door.

Mrs Robinson   I want to say something first.

Benjamin   Jesus Christ.

Mrs Robinson   Benjamin, I want you to know that I'm available to you . . .

Benjamin   Oh, my God . . .

Mrs Robinson   I want you to know you can call me up any time you want and we'll make some kind of arrangement.

Benjamin   Let me out.

Mrs Robinson   Do you understand what I said?

Benjamin   Yes! Yes! Let me out!

Mrs Robinson   Because I find you very attractive, and any time . . .

Mr Robinson (*off*)   Judith!

A moment, then **Mrs Robinson** *strides into the bathroom, grabbing her dress.* **Benjamin** *stares at the door as footsteps approach up the stairs.*

Mr Robinson (*off*)   Judith?

At the last moment, **Benjamin** *unlocks the door.*

Mr Robinson (*off*)   Benjamin?

And opens it.

Mr Robinson   Ah hah!

Benjamin   Ha hah!

Mr Robinson   Man of the moment.

Benjamin   Mr Robinson.

Mr Robinson   Have you seen my squiffy little wife?

Benjamin   I thought you were going to the airport.

Mr Robinson   I turned on the radio and lucky I did. The pilots came out in support of the cabin crews and nothing's flying out until morning. You know how much a stewardess thinks she's worth?

Benjamin   No I don't.

Mr Robinson   I never saw one didn't think she was God's gift. Wait a minute; that's not stewardesses, that's women, period. Know what I mean?

Benjamin   Yes.

Mr Robinson   Where is she?

Benjamin   Er . . . she's in the bathroom. She felt unwell.

Mr Robinson   She puke?

Benjamin   Well, she . . . I don't know.

Mr Robinson   She drinks so little, you understand. So when she drinks . . . Judith? Are you throwing up?

Mrs Robinson   I wasn't, but I might.

Mr Robinson   I've come to take you home.

Mrs Robinson   Give me a few minutes.

Mr Robinson   Is anything wrong? You look a little shaken up.

Benjamin   No, I'm just – I'm just – I'm just a little worried about my immediate future.

Mr Robinson   Ben, how old are you now?

Benjamin   I'll be twenty-one next week.

Mr Robinson   That's a hell of a good age to be.

Benjamin   Thank you.

Mr Robinson   I wish I was that age again. Because Ben?

Benjamin   What?

Mr Robinson   You'll never be young again.

Benjamin   I know.

Mr Robinson   Ben, can I say something to you?

Benjamin   Plastics?

Mr Robinson   No, Ben. I want to give you a bit of friendly advice.

Benjamin   I'd like to hear it.

Mr Robinson   I think you should take it a little easier than you seem to be. Have a good time with the girls and so forth. Sow a few wild oats. Because Ben, you're going to spend most of your life worrying. But right now you're young. Don't start worrying yet, for God's sake.

Benjamin   No.

Mr Robinson   Before you know it you'll find a nice little girl and settle down and have a damn fine life but until then try to make up a little for all the mistakes you're gonna make down the line. And while you're at it, make up for a few of mine.

Benjamin   I will, sir.

Mrs Robinson *comes out of the bathroom.*

Mr Robinson   I was just telling Ben here to sow a few wild oats. You think that's sound advice?

Mrs Robinson   Yes, I think that's sound advice.

Mr Robinson   You look like the kind of guy that has to fight them off.

Mrs Robinson   Are we going?

Mr Robinson   Say, when does Elaine get down from Berkeley?

Mrs Robinson   Saturday.

Mr Robinson   Ben, I want you to give her a call. Not that she's *any* girl, if you know what I'm saying?

Benjamin   I think I do.

Mr Robinson   Elaine's a wonderful girl. She's the sort of girl you'd only ever want to treat just right, you understand.

Benjamin   Yes I do.

Mr Robinson   I just know you two would hit it off really well. Wouldn't they?

Mrs Robinson   What?

Mr Robinson   Ben and Elaine. They'd like each other.

Mrs Robinson   I'm sure.

Benjamin's *mother comes in.*

Mom   Oh, you found each other.

Mr Robinson   We certainly did.

Mom   A shame about your trip, but nice you get to drive home.

Mrs Robinson   Good night, Olive.

Mom   Oh.

Mrs Robinson   Good night Benjamin.

Benjamin   Good night.

Mrs Robinson *leaves.*

Mr Robinson   Be seeing you, Ben. Olive.

Mom   Good night, Hal.

Mr Robinson *leaves.* **Benjamin** *puts on some sneakers.*

Mom   What are you putting on, Ben? Ben, it's a party; you can't wear those old things.

Benjamin   I'm not coming to the party, Mom.

Mom   Then what are you doing?

Benjamin   I'm leaving home.

Mom   What?

Benjamin   I'm leaving home. I'm clearing out.

Mom   You're going away?

Benjamin   That's right.

Mom   You're taking a trip?

Benjamin   That is right.

Mom   Well, where are you going?

Benjamin   I'm going on the road.

Mom   On the road?

Benjamin   I believe that's the conventional terminology.

Mom   You mean you're just going to pack your bag and go?

Benjamin   I'm not taking any bags.

Mom   What?

Benjamin   I'm taking what I have on.

Mom   Are you serious?

Benjamin   Yes.

Mom   Well, how much money are you taking?

Benjamin   Ten dollars.

Mom   Well, how long will you be gone?

Benjamin   Maybe five years. Maybe ten. I don't know.

Benjamin's *father comes in.*

Dad   Ben, you get your sorry ass down those stairs right now. (*To his wife.*) What's the matter with you?

Mom   Ben, you tell your father, because he's not going to let you do this.

Dad   Do what?

Benjamin   I'm going on a trip.

Mom   He's not taking any clothes. It's nine o'clock at night and he has ten dollars in his pocket and he's . . .

Dad   He's what?

Mom   He's going to do the road.

Dad   He's what?

Benjamin   I'm leaving.

Dad   You're what?

Mom   Ask him where he's going.

Benjamin   I don't know where I'm going.

Mom   He's going God knows where and he's leaving tonight.

Dad   He's what?

Mom   Tell him he's doing no such thing.

Dad   You're doing what?

Benjamin   I'm heading out. Across the country. Around the world. If I can get the papers, the passport, the whatever you need. I'll go right around the world.

Dad   You're gonna bum around the world?

Benjamin   I'm gonna work. I'm gonna meet a lot of interesting people. I'm through with all this.

Dad   All what?

Benjamin   All this. I don't know what it is but I'm sick of it. I want something else.

Dad   Well what the hell else do you want?

Benjamin   You know what I want?

Dad   No, son, I do not.

Benjamin   I want simple people. I want simple honest people that can't even read or write their own name. I want to spend my life with those sort of people.

Dad   Ben . . .

Benjamin   Farmers. Truck drivers. Ordinary people who don't have big houses. Who don't have swimming pools.

Dad   Don't get carried away now, son.

Benjamin   Real people, Dad.

Mom   Aren't we real?

Dad   You have a romantic notion here, Ben.

Benjamin   Real people like Gramps. You remember his hands?

Dad   Your grandfather built half of Toledo.

Benjamin   If you want the cliché Dad, I am going out to spend some time with the real people of this country.

Benjamin's *father thinks, then takes out his pocketbook and gives* **Benjamin** *the contents.*

Dad   I want you to take this.

Benjamin   I don't want it.

Dad   Here.

Benjamin   No.

Dad   Take it.

Benjamin   I won't.

His father puts it in **Benjamin**'s *pocket.*

Thank you.

Mom   So do we approve of this?

Dad   Do we *approve*? Son, lets you and I walk down those stairs. Let's show that bunch of . . . *grotesques* down there just what Benjamin Braddock is made of.

Benjamin   OK.

Dad   OK?

Benjamin   OK.

Dad   Call collect if you get into trouble.

Benjamin   I will.

They make for the door.

Mom   You have your father's approval, Ben.

Benjamin   I know.

Mom   Do you think you might be back by Saturday?

Dad   By Saturday? Heck no, he won't be back by Saturday.

He and **Benjamin** *laugh together.*

Benjamin   Why would I be back by Saturday?

Mom   Well, I invited the Robinsons over for dinner.

Benjamin   Well, I won't be back by Saturday.

Lights fade.

Scene Two

The same. Early morning. **Benjamin** *on the bed, grimy and exhausted. His father in a bathrobe.*

Dad   So, you're back.

Benjamin   I'm back.

Dad   Looks like you got a little beard started there.

Benjamin   It comes off tomorrow.

Dad   Well, how are you?

Benjamin   Tired.

Dad   You're all tired out.

Benjamin   That's right.

Dad   Well, two weeks.

Benjamin   No. Nine days.

Dad   That's a fair amount of time. How far did you get?

Benjamin   I don't know. Caluha. One of those towns.

Dad   Well, that's where the big fire is. You must have seen it.

Benjamin   Dad, I'm so tired I can't think.

Dad   How much did you spend?

Benjamin   Some.

Dad   Did you get some work?

Benjamin   Yes.

Dad   What kind of work?

Benjamin   Dad . . .

Dad   Come on Ben, I'm interested in this.

Benjamin   I fought the fire.

Dad   That big fire up there? You fought it?

Benjamin   That's right.

Dad   Well that's right up there by Shasta. You must have been right up there by Shasta country. That's beautiful country.

Benjamin   Yes it is.

Dad   How much they pay you on a deal like that?

Benjamin   Five an hour.

Dad   Five dollars an hour?

Benjamin   That's right.

Dad   They give you the equipment and you go in and you try to put out the flames?

Benjamin   That's right.

Dad   Well what about the Indians? I was reading they transported some Indians up there from Arizona. Professional fire-fighters. Did you see some of them?

Benjamin   I saw some Indians, yes.

Dad   This is exciting. What else happened?

Benjamin   Nothing.

Dad   Where did you stay?

Benjamin   Hotels.

Dad   Expensive hotels?

Benjamin   Cheap hotels.

Dad   Talk to a lot of interesting people?

Benjamin   No.

Dad   You didn't?

Benjamin   I talked to a lot of people. None of them were particularly interesting.

Dad   Did you talk to some Indians?

Benjamin   Yes.

Dad   They speak English?

Benjamin   Yes.

Dad   Well, what else did you . . .

Benjamin   Dad, the trip was a complete waste of time and I'd rather not talk about it. It was a bore.

Dad   Well it doesn't sound too boring if you were up there throwing water on that fire.

Benjamin   It was a boring fire.

Dad   Well, tell me about it Ben. What kind of people did you bump into? What kind of people gave you rides?

Benjamin   Queers.

Dad What?

Benjamin Queers usually stopped. I averaged about five queers a day. One queer I had to hit in the face and jump out his car.

Dad Homosexuals?

Benjamin Ever met a queer Indian?

Dad A what?

Benjamin Ever had a queer Indian try to jump you while you're trying to keep your clothes from burning up?

Dad Did this happen?

Benjamin Mainly I talked. I talked to farmers.

Dad What about?

Benjamin Crops.

Dad Crops?

Benjamin That's all they know to talk about.

Dad And that's who you talked to?

Benjamin I talked to tramps. I talked to drunks. I talked to whores.

Dad Whores?

Benjamin Yes. I talked to whores. One of them swiped my watch.

Dad A whore stole your wristwatch?

Benjamin Yes.

Dad While you were . . . talking to her?

Benjamin No.

Dad Then you – then you spent the night with a whore?

Benjamin There were a few whores included in the tour, yes.

Dad   More than one?

Benjamin   It gets to be a habit.

Dad   How many?

Benjamin   I don't remember. There was one in a hotel. There was one at her house. There was one in the back of a bar.

Dad   Is this true, Ben?

Benjamin   One in a field.

Dad   A field?

Benjamin   A cow pasture. It was about three in the morning and there was ice in the grass and cows walking around us.

Dad   Ben, this doesn't sound too good.

Benjamin   It wasn't.

Dad   I guess you did quite a bit of drinking on this trip.

Benjamin   Well, it's not too likely I'd spend the night with a stinking whore in a field full of frozen manure if I was stone-cold sober, now is it?

Benjamin's *mother enters.*

Mom   Here's coffee. Now, let's hear all about this trip.

Dad   I think Ben needs some sleep.

Mom   Where did you go? What did you do?

Dad   Let's go down and leave him be.

Benjamin   I have to take a shower.

Benjamin *leaves the room.*

Mom   Welcome home, Ben . . . Is something wrong?

Dad   Leave the boy alone. He's fine.

Mom   Did something happen?

Dad   Nothing happened.

Mom   He seems a little disillusioned.

Dad   Disillusioned?

Mom   Increasingly disillusioned. Today's young people . . .

Dad   What the hell would you know about *disillusioned*?

He leaves. She follows.

Mom   I read in the digest that today's young people . . .

Dad   Don't talk to *me* about disillusioned.

Benjamin *appears in a phone booth.*

Benjamin   Mrs Robinson? This is Ben Braddock. Hi. I was wondering if we could . . . no! No. If we could meet for a *drink* or . . . Or something. Well . . . Where would you suggest?

Scene Three

Lobby of the Taft Hotel. Well appointed. Door USR becomes entrance from street, door DSL becomes a reception desk. **Benjamin***, hair slicked, rigid with false nonchalance, walks in. As he looks around him, the* **Desk Clerk** *looks up.*

Desk Clerk   Good evening, sir.

Benjamin   Good evening.

Desk Clerk   Can I help you?

Benjamin   No thank you.

Desk Clerk   Will you be wanting a room, sir?

Benjamin   No. No, thank you.

A phone rings just off-stage. The **Desk Clerk** *disappears to answer it.* **Mrs Robinson** *walks in.*

Mrs Robinson   Hello, Benjamin.

Benjamin   Oh. Hello.

Mrs Robinson   How are you?

Benjamin   Very well. Thank you.

Mrs Robinson   Did you get us a room?

Benjamin   What?

Mrs Robinson   Have you gotten us a room yet?

Benjamin   I haven't, no.

Mrs Robinson   Do you want to?

Benjamin   Well, I . . . I mean I could. Or we could just talk. We could have a drink and just talk if you'd rather I'd be perfectly happy to . . .

Mrs Robinson   Do you want me to get it?

Benjamin   You? No. No, I'll – now?

Mrs Robinson   Yes. Why don't you get it now?

Benjamin   Right now?

Mrs Robinson   Why don't you?

Benjamin   I will then.

Benjamin *crosses to the desk. Taps the bell, which rings uncomfortably loud. He muffles it. The* **Desk Clerk** *returns.*

Desk Clerk   Yes sir?

Benjamin   I changed my mind. I'd like a room, please.

Desk Clerk   A single room or a double room?

Benjamin   A single. Just for myself, please.

Desk Clerk   Will you sign your name, please.

Benjamin *signs a card, crumples it, puts it in his pocket and signs a second card.*

Desk Clerk   Is something wrong, sir?

Benjamin   No. Nothing.

Desk Clerk   Very good sir. We have a single room on the fifth floor. Twelve dollars. Would that be suitable?

Benjamin   Yes, that would be suitable.

Benjamin *gets his wallet out.*

Desk Clerk   You can pay when you check out, sir.

Benjamin   Oh, right. Excuse me.

Desk Clerk   Do you have any luggage?

Benjamin   Yes I do.

Desk Clerk   Where is it?

Benjamin   What?

Desk Clerk   Your luggage.

Benjamin   Well, it's in the car. It's out there in the car.

Desk Clerk   I'll have the porter bring it in.

He rings for the porter.

Benjamin   Oh no . . .

Benjamin *puts his hand over the bell. The* **Desk Clerk** *accidentally thumps* **Benjamin**'*s hand.*

Desk Clerk   Sir?

Benjamin   I mean I'd rather not go to the trouble of bringing it all in. I just have a toothbrush. I can get it myself. If that's all right.

Desk Clerk   Of course. I'll have a porter show you the room.

Benjamin   No, that's all right. I just have the toothbrush to carry up and I think I can handle it myself.

Desk Clerk   Whatever you say, sir.

He hands **Benjamin** *the key.* **Mrs Robinson** *comes over.*

Mrs Robinson   Is everything all right?

Benjamin   Oh, yes. Thank you. This is er . . . This is my, er . . . Did you get it?

Mrs Robinson   Did I get what?

Benjamin   My toothbrush? I left it in the car.

The phone rings again.

Desk Clerk   Excuse me.

The **Desk Clerk** *leaves.*

Mrs Robinson   Shall we go up?

Benjamin   Well, yes. But um – well, there might be a problem.

Mrs Robinson   What's that?

Benjamin   I got a single room and he um . . . the man . . .

Mrs Robinson   The clerk.

Benjamin   The desk clerk. I think he'll be suspicious now.

Mrs Robinson   Well, do you want to go up alone first?

Benjamin   May I? I mean yes. I would. I mean, I don't know what their policy is here.

Mrs Robinson   I'll be up in ten minutes.

Benjamin   Ten minutes. Right. OK.

Benjamin *walks away.*

Mrs Robinson   Benjamin.

Benjamin   Yes?

Mrs Robinson   Aren't you forgetting something?

Benjamin   Mm? Oh. Mrs Robinson, I really am very grateful for— (this opportunity).

Mrs Robinson   The room number, Benjamin.

Benjamin   Oh, it's um . . . five-eleven.

The **Desk Clerk** *returns.*

Desk Clerk   I beg your pardon.

Benjamin   That's fine. We're . . . I'm just . . .

Desk Clerk   Would a double room be more suitable?

Benjamin   Um . . .

Mrs Robinson   Thank you.

Desk Clerk   I think you'll find it altogether more spacious.

He and **Benjamin** *switch keys.*

Benjamin   Thank you.

Mrs Robinson   And some champagne?

Desk Clerk   No problem at all madam. The elevator's just there.

Benjamin   Thank you.

Desk Clerk   Thank *you.* Goodnight, Mr Gladstone.

The lights change suddenly, isolating **Mrs Robinson** *and* **Benjamin** *in an illuminated square representing the rising elevator. The scene changes in the surrounding darkness.*

Benjamin   You seem very . . .

Mrs Robinson   What?

Benjamin   Er . . .

Mrs Robinson   Do you think I've done this before?

Benjamin   Have you?

Mrs Robinson   What do you think?

Benjamin   I don't know.

Mrs Robinson   There's only one right answer Benjamin, and that wasn't it.

Ben   I'm nervous.

Mrs Robinson   Try small talk.

The lights fade swiftly.

Scene Four

Room 515, the Taft Hotel. Doors to corridor, bathroom and closet. **Benjamin** *standing with his hands in his pockets.* **Mrs Robinson**   *sitting on the bed. She has champagne.*

Benjamin   About that high. Which may not seem very high, but that's quite high. For actual flames. If you're actually in them . . .

Mrs Robinson   So did you put it out?

Benjamin   Personally?

Mrs Robinson   You and the Indians.

Benjamin   Yes, we did. And the firemen. We eventually – put it out.

Mrs Robinson   I'm impressed. I'll get undressed now. Is that all right?

Benjamin   Sure. Fine.

She stands up, takes a last pull on her cigarette and turns to put it out. **Benjamin** *moves closer and kisses her. When their lips part she exhales her cigarette smoke. Then she unbuttons her blouse.*

Benjamin   Do you—

Mrs Robinson   What?

Benjamin   I mean, do you want me to just stand here? I don't know what you want me to do.

Mrs Robinson   Why don't you watch.

Benjamin   Oh. Sure. Thank you.

She takes off her blouse. He puts his hand on her breast. She notices a smudge on her blouse, and rubs it off. He takes his hand away.

Mrs Robinson   Would you get me a hanger?

Benjamin   Certainly.

He goes to the closet.

A wood one?

Mrs Robinson   What?

Benjamin   They have wire ones or wooden ones.

Mrs Robinson   A wooden one is fine.

He struggles to get a wooden hanger out, but they're fixed in. She takes off her skirt. He returns with a wire hanger.

Benjamin   The wood ones are fixed to the rail.

Mrs Robinson   Would this be easier for you in the dark?

Benjamin   No.

Mrs Robinson   Are you sure?

Benjamin   Yes.

She gives him the hanger with her skirt on it, which he takes to the closet. She's reaching to undo her bra when he begins to bang his head against the closet door.

Mrs Robinson   Benjamin?

Benjamin   I can't do this. Mrs Robinson, I cannot do this!

Mrs Robinson   You don't want to do this?

Benjamin   You have no idea how much. I do. And don't. I do, but I can't. Now I'm just, I'm sorry I called you up but I—

Mrs Robinson   Benjamin—

Benjamin   I mean don't you see? Don't you see how this is the worst thing I could possibly do?

Mrs Robinson   Is that why you're doing it?

Benjamin   No. I just – Mrs Robinson, could I take you to a movie?

Mrs Robinson   Are you trying to be funny?

Benjamin   No! But I don't know what to say, because I've got you up here and now I—

Mrs Robinson   You don't know what to do with me.

Benjamin   Well, I know I can't do this!

Mrs Robinson   Benjamin, do you find me desirable?

Benjamin   Mrs Robinson, you are the most attractive of all my parents' friends. And that includes Mrs Terhune. I find you more than adequately desirable, but for God's sake; can you imagine my parents? Can you imagine what my parents would say if they saw us in here right now?

Mrs Robinson   What *would* they say?

Benjamin   I have no idea Mrs Robinson, but for God's sake. They've brought me up. They've made a good life for me. I think they deserve something a little better than this.

Mrs Robinson *nods.*

Benjamin   I mean, this has nothing to do with you. But I respect my parents, and I appreciate what they've . . .

Mrs Robinson   Benjamin?

Benjamin   Yes?

Mrs Robinson   Can I asked you a personal question?

Benjamin   Ask me anything you want.

Mrs Robinson   Is this your first time?

Benjamin   Is this what?

Mrs Robinson   It is, isn't it? This is your first time.

Benjamin   Well, that's a laugh, Mrs Robinson. That really is a laugh.

He laughs weakly.

Mrs Robinson   Well, it's nothing to be ashamed of—

Benjamin   Are you kidding?

Mrs Robinson   It's perfectly natural to be nervous if it's your first time—

Benjamin   Now wait a minute.

Mrs Robinson   Just because you're a little inadequate in one area it doesn't mean—

Benjamin   Inadequate!

Mrs Robinson   Well I guess I'd better be— (going)

Benjamin   Stay on the bed! Sit on the bed. Stay there.

Benjamin *tears off his clothes, loses his balance, falls over.*

Blackout.

Scene Five

The same. Music. The light through the blinds plays a fugue of passing time as **Benjamin** *and* **Mrs Robinson** *make love, unseen beneath the sheets. Summer days come and go. Dawn breaks and the love-making forms a tableau as the closet door (which was also* **Benjamin***'s bedroom door) opens and we see* **Benjamin***'s mother beyond it. The lighting indicates we are in two places and two times at once.*

Mom   Ben? It's nearly eleven o'clock. It's a beautiful day, Ben. Are you going to spend all summer in bed?

She closes the door. **Benjamin** *climaxes and the lovers change positions. More time passes until the door opens again and we see* **Benjamin**'s *father beyond it.*

Dad   Ben, will you please get up off that bed and clean the pool or trim the lawn, or do *something* for Heaven's sake. You come in at all hours and your scholarship, Ben. When are you going to take up your scholarship?!

Dad *disappears and* **Benjamin** *climaxes again. The lovers change positions once more,* **Mrs Robinson** *firmly guiding* **Benjamin**'s *head beneath the covers. Finally the lights settle to early evening and* **Benjamin** *emerges.*

Mrs Robinson   Don't stop. Benjamin? What's wrong?

Benjamin   Mrs Robinson, do you think we could have a conversation?

Mrs Robinson   A conversation?

Benjamin   Yes.

Mrs Robinson   Why?

Benjamin   Well we've been coming here and doing this for a couple of months now and we never seem to talk about anything. I just wondered if you'd mind very much if we had a conversation. I mean we're not stupid people are we?

Mrs Robinson   I don't know.

Benjamin   Well we're not, but all we ever do is come up here and throw off our clothes and leap into bed together.

Mrs Robinson   Are you tired of it?

Benjamin   I'm not, no. But do you think we could liven it up with a few words now and then?

Mrs Robinson   What do you want to talk about, darling?

Benjamin   Anything. Anything at all.

Mrs Robinson   Do you want to tell me about your childhood?

Benjamin   No I don't.

Mrs Robinson   Kiss me then.

Benjamin   No. Now we are going to do this thing. We are going to have a conversation. Think of a topic.

Mrs Robinson   How about art?

Benjamin   Art. That's a good subject. You start it off.

Mrs Robinson   I don't know anything about it.

Benjamin   You what?

Mrs Robinson   Do you?

Benjamin   Well, yes I do. I know quite a bit about it.

Mrs Robinson   Go ahead then.

Benjamin   Are you interested in modern art or classical art?

Mrs Robinson   Neither.

Benjamin   You're not interested in art?

Mrs Robinson   No.

Benjamin   Then why do you want to talk about it?

Mrs Robinson   I don't. Could we go back to what we were doing?

Benjamin   No. Think of another topic.

Mrs Robinson   Why don't you tell me what you did today?

Benjamin   This is pathetic.

Mrs Robinson   What did you do?

Benjamin   I got up around twelve. I ate breakfast. I had some beers. I went out to the pool. I blew air in my raft, I put the raft in the water, I floated on the raft. I ate dinner, I watched two quiz shows, then I came here. What did you do?

Mrs Robinson   I got up.

Benjamin   Is that all?

Mrs Robinson   I came here.

Benjamin   What did you do in between?

Mrs Robinson   I read a novel.

Benjamin   An entire novel?

Mrs Robinson   Five or six pages.

Benjamin   What was the novel?

Mrs Robinson   I can't remember.

Benjamin   Is that all you did?

Mrs Robinson   I fixed dinner for my husband.

Benjamin   There! That's something we can have a conversation about! Your husband. I mean I don't know anything about how you work this, how you get out of the house at night, what are the risks involved.

Mrs Robinson   There's no risk.

Benjamin   How do you get out of the house?

Mrs Robinson   I walk out.

Benjamin   You walk right out the door?

Mrs Robinson   That's right

Benjamin   What do you tell him?

Mrs Robinson   Benjamin, this isn't a very interesting topic.

Benjamin   Please, tell me.

Mrs Robinson   He's out all day. He comes home, he takes two Seconal, then it's tomorrow.

Benjamin   So I guess you don't sleep together or anything?

Mrs Robinson   No, we don't.

Benjamin   How long has this been going on?

Mrs Robinson   Four or five years.

Benjamin   Are you kidding me?

Mrs Robinson   No.

Benjamin   You have not slept with your husband for four or five years? Man, this is interesting.

Mrs Robinson   Calm down, Benjamin.

Benjamin   We're talking, Mrs Robinson. We are talking.

Mrs Robinson   We certainly are.

Benjamin   So you don't love him. You wouldn't say you—

Mrs Robinson   I think we've talked enough.

Benjamin   But you loved him once, I assume. When you first knew him.

Mrs Robinson   Well, no.

Benjamin   Never?

Mrs Robinson   I never did. Now would you please—

Benjamin   Well, wait a minute. You married him.

Mrs Robinson   Yes I did.

Benjamin   Well why did you do that?

Mrs Robinson   Let's see if you can guess.

Benjamin   His money?

Mrs Robinson   Think really hard, Benjamin.

Benjamin   You had to? I mean you *had* to? Did you have to?

Mrs Robinson   Don't tell Elaine.

Benjamin   You really had to.

Mrs Robinson   Are you shocked?

Benjamin   Well, I never thought of you and Mr Robinson as the sort of people who, I mean . . . how did it happen? Do you feel like telling me the circumstances?

Mrs Robinson   Not particularly.

Benjamin   Was he a law student at the time?

Mrs Robinson   Yes.

Benjamin   And you were a student also?

Mrs Robinson   Yes.

Benjamin   What was your major?

Mrs Robinson   Benjamin . . .

Benjamin   I'm interested. What was your major subject?

Mrs Robinson   Art.

Benjamin   Art?

Mrs Robinson   Art.

Benjamin   How did you get pregnant?

Mrs Robinson   Pardon me?

Benjamin   Did he take you to a hotel?

Mrs Robinson   Benjamin . . .

Benjamin   I'm curious.

Mrs Robinson   We did it in his car.

Benjamin *is delighted.*

Benjamin   In his car!? Oh boy. In a car?! What kind of car?

Mrs Robinson   What?

Benjamin   Do you remember the make of car?

Mrs Robinson   My God.

Benjamin   Really. I want to know.

Mrs Robinson   It was a Ford, Benjamin.

Benjamin   A Ford? A Ford! Goddammit, a Ford! That's great.

Mrs Robinson   Benjamin, I'm beginning to think sleeping with younger men may have its disadvantages.

Benjamin   So old Elaine Robinson got started in a Ford.

Mrs Robinson   Don't talk about Elaine.

Benjamin   Don't talk about Elaine?

Mrs Robinson   No.

Benjamin   That reminds me.

Mrs Robinson   What?

Benjamin   I have to talk about her.

Mrs Robinson   I don't want you to.

Benjamin   I have to. I've been meaning to all night. I have to talk about Elaine.

Mrs Robinson   What about her?

Benjamin   I have to see her. I have to go out with Elaine. I have to go on a date with Elaine.

Mrs Robinson   You have to what?

Benjamin   You see Mr Robinson called my dad and my dad said I was still hanging around the house and they arranged that I should take out Elaine.

Mrs Robinson   Benjamin, don't you dare.

Benjamin   I have no choice. It turned into a whole big thing about my wasting my life and watching TV all the time and he, my dad, said if I didn't take out Elaine he'd cut off my allowance and throw me out the house. He became irrational, so I said OK. I'll just take her to a movie. Why are you getting so upset?

Mrs Robinson   I'm not getting upset, Benjamin, I am telling you you are not to see Elaine.

Benjamin   Are you jealous of her? Are you afraid I might like her?

Mrs Robinson   No.

Benjamin   Well then what?

Mrs Robinson   Drop it, Benjamin.

Benjamin   I want to know why you feel so strongly about this.

Mrs Robinson   I have my reasons!

Benjamin   Then let's hear your reasons, Mrs Robinson. Because I think I know what they are.

She ducks beneath the covers.

Your daughter shouldn't associate with the likes of me, should she? I'm not good enough for her to associate with, am I? That's the reason, isn't it? I'm a dirty degenerate, aren't I? I'm good enough for you but I'm too slimy to associate with your daughter. That's it, isn't it? Isn't it?

Mrs Robinson   YES!

Benjamin   You go to hell.

He gets dressed.

You go straight to hell, Mrs Robinson.

Mrs Robinson   Benjamin.

Benjamin   Do you think I'm proud of myself? Do you think I'm proud of this?

Mrs Robinson   I wouldn't know.

Benjamin   Well, I'm not. No sir. I am not proud of spending my time in hotel rooms with a lascivious alcoholic.

Mrs Robinson   I see.

Benjamin   And if you think I come here for any reason beside pure boredom, then you're all wrong.

She nods.

Because . . . Mrs Robinson?

Mrs Robinson   What?

Benjamin   You make me sick! I make myself sick. This is the sickest, most perverted thing that ever happened to me and you do what you want but I'm getting the hell out.

A pause as he dresses.

Mrs Robinson   Do you mean those things?

Benjamin   Damn right I do.

Mrs Robinson   Well, I'm sorry.

Benjamin   Well, I'm sorry too, but that's the way it is.

Mrs Robinson   That's how you feel about me?

He nods.

That I'm a sick and disgusting person.

Benjamin   Now, don't start acting hurt, Mrs Robinson. You told me yourself you were an alcoholic. You lie there and call me trash, what do you expect me to say?

Mrs Robinson   Did I call you that?

Benjamin   You did. You lay there and told me I was not good enough for your daughter.

Mrs Robinson   If that's the impression you got Benjamin, I would like to apologise. You're as good a person as she is. It's just that under the circumstances I don't think you'd be right for each other.

Benjamin   I'm as good as she is?

Mrs Robinson   You're as good as she is. Brighter, certainly. In many ways her equal.

She gets up and dresses.

Benjamin   What are you doing?

Mrs Robinson   Well, it's obvious you don't want me around any more.

Benjamin   Well, I was kind of upset.

Mrs Robinson   I can understand why I might disgust you.

Benjamin   No, no. I like you.

Mrs Robinson   I should have realised how sickening this might be for you . . .

Benjamin   It's not! I like it. I like it very much. I look forward to it. It's the one thing I have to look forward to.

Mrs Robinson   You don't have to say that.

Benjamin   I wouldn't say it if it wasn't true.

Mrs Robinson   But you think we should stop seeing each other?

Benjamin   No.

Mrs Robinson   Shall we go back to bed then?

Benjamin   Yes. OK.

Mrs Robinson   I'd like that.

Benjamin   I just need the bathroom.

He goes into the bathroom.

Mrs Robinson   And you won't go out with Elaine.

Benjamin   I'm going to lose my allowance.

Mrs Robinson   Benjamin!

Benjamin   I have no intention of going out with Elaine.

Mrs Robinson   Give me your word.

Benjamin   This is absurd.

Mrs Robinson   Promise me.

Benjamin   I promise! I will not go out with Elaine!

Mrs Robinson   Well, good. Immature son of a bitch.

Blackout.

Elaine *appears downstage, waiting on a downtown street corner.*
Shadows and neon.

Elaine   Oh, thank you no. I'm waiting for someone. Well,
thank you. No. No, I'm fine. I'm waiting for someone.
Pardon me? No!

Benjamin *enters.*

Benjamin   Hi.

Elaine   Oh, hi.

Benjamin   Am I late?

Elaine   Oh, no.

Benjamin   Good.

Elaine   Where are we going?

Benjamin   Inside.

Elaine   Oh. Well . . . that's nice.

Scene Six

The Club Renaissance. A tacky Hollywood bar. A jukebox USR. Two men sit with a pitcher of beer and one of their heads on the table. **Benjamin** *sits with* **Elaine**. *She looks childlike and out of place. The* **Waiter** *passes.*

Elaine   What is this place?

Benjamin   It's a very lively place. It livens up eventually. You like beer?

Elaine   Um, well . . .

Benjamin   Could we have two beers, please?

Elaine   . . . yes.

Benjamin   Would you like some dinner?

Elaine   I'd love some.

Benjamin   Could we have a menu?

Waiter   Dinner for two, sir?

Benjamin   No, just for her.

Elaine   Aren't you eating?

Benjamin   I'm not hungry, if it's all the same to you.

Elaine   Oh. Oh well.

A difficult pause.

Elaine   I heard you got a scholarship.

Benjamin   I don't want to teach.

Elaine   Oh, but a good teacher is a rare and wonderful thing.

Benjamin   That's what my parents think.

Elaine   Well, it's true.

Benjamin   That's not what the world thinks. The world thinks you failed before you began.

The **Waiter** *brings beer.*

Elaine   So do you have a job lined up?

Benjamin   No.

Elaine   Do you have anything in mind?

Benjamin   No.

Elaine   Would you like to guess what I saw last month?

Benjamin   What did you see?

Elaine   You'll never guess.

Benjamin   Then I won't try. What was it?

Elaine   I saw the *Mona Lisa*.

Benjamin   Did you?

Elaine   The *Mona Lisa*. It's on loan to the Washington Museum and my room-mate Diane and I went on the civil rights march? There were two hundred thousand people. We were lucky to get a hotel room and the day after we went to see the *Mona Lisa*.

Benjamin   Was she smiling?

Elaine   Well of course she was. Aren't you interested in beautiful things?

A **Stripper** *enters and puts a dime in the jukebox. Music begins. She flicks a switch to dim the room and another to light some tacky coloured spots.*

Elaine   Oh.

Elaine *turns. The* **Stripper** *drops her robe and starts her act. One of the men slaps the other on the shoulder. He lifts his head.* **Elaine** *realises what she's watching and turns around again, bowing her head.*

Elaine   Could we get a table somewhere else?

Benjamin   I didn't make a reservation.

Elaine *takes a sip of a drink, then pushes it to* **Benjamin**.

Elaine   Would you drink this for me, please.

Benjamin   Why don't you watch the show?

Elaine   Benjamin, do you dislike me?

Benjamin   What?

Elaine   Do you dislike me for some reason?

Benjamin   No, why should I?

Elaine   I don't know.

The **Stripper** *swings her tassels to desultory applause.*

Benjamin   You're missing a great effect here.

Elaine *looks*.

Benjamin   How about that?

Elaine *turns back.*

Benjamin   Could you do that?

The **Stripper** *comes up behind* **Elaine** *and tousles her hair with her tassels. The men laugh. One applauds.* **Elaine** *starts to cry.* **Benjamin**'s *discomfort grows until he suddenly leaps up and pulls the plug on the jukebox.*

Man   Hey!

Benjamin   I'm sorry.

Stripper   What do you think you're doing?

Benjamin   I'm sorry. My friend's not feeling well.

He offers her a dime. She just looks at him.

Sorry.

He offers her some crumpled dollars, which she takes.

Stripper   Excuse me if I earn a living.

Glances at **Elaine***, then strides away.*

Man   Hey, babe!

Stripper   Back room, kiddo.

She leaves. One man's head sinks back down on the table. The other looks at **Benjamin***.*

Man   What's the matter with ya?

Benjamin   I'm sorry.

He follows the **Stripper***.* **Benjamin** *returns to* **Elaine***, who is clinging to her chair.*

Elaine   Would you take me home now, please?

Benjamin   I'm sorry.

Elaine   Could you get the cheque, please?

Benjamin   Elaine, listen . . .

Elaine   Please, just take me home.

Benjamin   I have to tell you something. This whole idea of the date and everything. It was my parents' idea. They forced me into it.

Elaine   Oh. That's nice of you to tell me.

Benjamin   I'm not like this.

Elaine   Will you drive me home now, please?

Benjamin   Well, can't we have dinner or something?

Elaine   NO!

Music filters through from the back room.

Benjamin   Can we just sit somewhere and talk?

Elaine   I want to go home!

Benjamin   I want to talk to you first.

Elaine   Please, Benjamin.

Benjamin   Could you stop crying, please?

Elaine   No I couldn't.

Benjamin   But could you try?

Elaine   No.

Benjamin   This is embarrassing. You want to leave?

Elaine   No.

Benjamin   You said you wanted to.

Elaine   I changed my mind.

Benjamin   Let's go outside.

Elaine   This is where you took me, Benjamin. If it's all the same to you, this is where I'll cry.

Benjamin   I want you to know I hate myself.

Elaine   Thank you for saving me the trouble.

Benjamin   I've been going through a difficult time lately.

Elaine   I'm sorry to hear it.

Benjamin   My life is bullshit.

Elaine   Your life is what?

Benjamin   Well, bullshit.

Elaine   How can you say that?

Benjamin   It's what I think.

Elaine   Life is bullshit?

Benjamin   My whole life.

Elaine   Then I feel sorry for you.

Benjamin   I feel sorry for myself.

Elaine   I don't believe I'm sitting here with a nihilist. I'm always being attached on to by nihilists. I hate nihilists. I try to avoid them.

Benjamin   Feel free to avoid me from now on.

Elaine   Have you ever read *The Fountainhead?*

Benjamin   No.

Elaine   Have you ever seen the *Mona Lisa?*

Benjamin   No.

Elaine   Well, I have.

Benjamin   I know you have.

Elaine   The world is full of wonderful things. How can you sit there and say life is bullshit?

Benjamin   I've had a very good education.

Elaine   Then be grateful. There are people fighting for an education in Alabama. Fighting state troopers for a good education. Do you think they think life is bullshit?

Benjamin   Very possibly.

Elaine   A monk just set fire to himself in Saigon . . .

Benjamin   Well, hey.

Elaine   Life is precious, Benjamin. How dare you. How dare you sit there and say life is bullshit. When you have so much. When whatever you want you could probably have.

Benjamin   You like your life?

Elaine   I *love* my life. Don't you?

Benjamin   Once, I guess. When I was a kid.

Elaine   What happeed?

Benjamin   It was unrequited.

Elaine   Well, nothing's perfect Benjamin. I'd have liked a nicer nose. I wish my mother didn't drink so much. I wish I'd never fallen out of that tree and broken my thumb because it so affects my fingering I'll probably never play the violin as well as I'd love to but that's about it for the bullshit,

Benjamin. It's only bullshit if you let it pile up. Heaven's in the details. Someone said that. I think Robert Frost said that.

The **Stripper** *returns having finished her act. Picks up her robe from somewhere near* **Elaine**.

Elaine   You have beautiful breasts.

The **Stripper** *looks at* **Elaine** *and* **Elaine** *looks right back.*

Stripper   Thank you.

Elaine   I'm sorry I cried.

Stripper   I'm sorry I made you.

She eyes **Benjamin**, *turns back to* **Elaine**.

Stripper   So, what, are you screwing him for practice?

Elaine *laughs, surprisingly loudly. The* **Stripper** *smiles.*

Stripper   OK, babe.

The **Stripper** *leaves.* **Elaine** *continues talking to* **Benjamin**.

Elaine   She's nice.

Ben   Nice?

Elaine   Nice people. I was in this diner with my room-mate Diane? And this guy came in with a goat on a rope and it turns out the reason he's got a little goat on a rope is he was thrown out the day before for bringing in his dog? But the point is Diane had stood up to leave when she saw the man walk in and she sat straight down again and said, Well if there's a goat I think I'll have dessert. And that's why I love Diane, because if you think like that you not only notice more little goats, you get more dessert. Will she dance again?

Benjamin   I don't think so.

Elaine   Then let's go!

She leaps up. **Benjamin** *follows her.*

Do you have a car?

Benjamin   No.

Elaine   Good. I love cabs. Don't you? And cab drivers? I think cab drivers are mostly fallen angels.

Benjamin *kisses her.*

Elaine   Why did you do that?

Benjamin   Your mouth. It's very beautiful.

Elaine   No it isn't.

Benjamin   Very *Mona Lisa*.

Elaine   No bullshit.

Benjamin *laughs.*

Benjamin   No bullshit?

Elaine   Well, don't do it again.

Benjamin   Don't you like me?

Elaine   You're cute Benjamin, but you're kind of morose.

Benjamin   I'm cute?

Elaine   Way too serious.

Benjamin   But cute?

Elaine   Yes.

Benjamin   How?

Elaine   I really have no idea.

Benjamin   Like a goat?

Elaine   Maybe.

Benjamin   So would you like to go somewhere and get some dessert?

Elaine   Way to go, Benjamin.

She smiles. Lights fade.

Scene Seven

The Robinsons' living room. Front door and stairs. **Benjamin** *waits anxious yet brash, spinning car keys on his finger.* **Mrs Robinson** *enters more quickly than she intended. A stony silence.*

Benjamin   Mrs Robinson, I hope you won't be offended if I say I think you're being a little melodramatic about this. Elaine and I are just going for a drive. I don't think there's any great crisis that necessitates any degree of acrimony here.

Mrs Robinson   Turn around and leave the house, Benjamin. Get back in your car and drive away.

Benjamin   What exactly are you trying to say, Mrs Robinson?

Mrs Robinson   I'm telling you never to see her again. Do I make myself clear?

Benjamin   Yes you do.

Mrs Robinson   Then the matter's closed.

Benjamin   No it's not, because I have no intention of following your orders, Mrs Robinson.

Mrs Robinson   Benjamin, if you think . . .

Benjamin   Why don't you tell me exactly what your objections are instead of . . .

Mrs Robinson   Elaine is a very simple girl. She is sweet, uncomplicated and thoroughly honest. And she is thoroughly sincere. And Benjamin, you are none of these things. You are a lot of things, but you add up to nothing.

Benjamin   What time does she usually get up?

Mrs Robinson   I don't think you need to worry about that.

Benjamin   I think we do. I think we have a date and I think she's expecting me.

Mrs Robinson   I could make things most unpleasant.

Benjamin   In what way would that be?

Mrs Robinson   To keep her away from you I would tell Elaine anything I had to.

A pause.

Benjamin   I don't believe you.

Mrs Robinson   Well, you'd better.

Benjamin   I don't think you would do that.

Mrs Robinson   You want to watch?

Benjamin   Would you do that? Mrs Robinson, I'm asking you not to do that. Please don't do that.

Mrs Robinson   Go home now.

Benjamin   Please, don't wreck it. I'm asking you please not to wreck it.

Mrs Robinson   Wreck it?

Benjamin   Please.

Mrs Robinson   Wreck what?

Benjamin *hangs his head.*

Mrs Robinson   Are you in love Benjamin? Do you have the audacity? The indecency?

Enter **Elaine** *in her dressing gown.*

Elaine   Benjamin?

Mrs Robinson   Elaine, go back upstairs.

Elaine   Why are you so early?

Benjamin   It's a beautiful day; would you like to get in the car?

Elaine   I'm not dressed.

Mrs Robinson   Go back upstairs, Elaine.

Benjamin   Get dressed, I'll wait down here.

Mrs Robinson   Benjamin was just leaving.

Benjamin   No he wasn't. No I'm not.

Elaine   Is something wrong?

Benjamin   I'll be right here.

Mrs Robinson   Benjamin's not feeling well.

Benjamin   I'm perfectly all right.

Elaine   I don't understand.

Benjamin   Get dressed, Elaine.

Mrs Robinson   Goodbye, Benjamin.

Elaine   Would someone please tell me what's going on?
Mother?

She looks at her mother. So does **Benjamin**. **Mrs Robinson**
looks at **Benjamin**, *then back at her daughter. Before she can speak,*
Benjamin *does.*

Benjamin   Elaine, I have something to tell you.

Mrs Robinson   Benjamin.

Benjamin   I have been having an affair. I have been
having an affair with an older woman.

Elaine   What are you talking about?

Mrs Robinson   Get dressed Elaine.

Benjamin   With a married woman.

Mrs Robinson   Benjamin's waiting to take you for a ride.

Benjamin   I just wanted you to know.

Elaine   Well, thank you. I'll get dressed.

She makes to leave, then stops dead. She slowly turns to her mother and **Benjamin**.

Oh my God.

Mrs Robinson   Elaine . . .

Elaine   Oh my God.

Benjamin   Listen, Elaine.

Elaine   Oh my God. Get out of here.

Benjamin   Elaine . . .

Elaine   Would you please? Oh my God. Oh my God. Would you please get out of here? My God.

Benjamin   Should I come back later?

Elaine *looks at him. He leaves. She looks at her mother.* **Mrs Robinson**'s *knees slowly buckle and she sits on the floor. Using ice and a shaker,* **Elaine** *fixes a vodka cocktail and gives it to her mother.* **Elaine** *returns to the shaker and pours the rest for herself. The glass is half empty, so she tops it up with vodka. Sits opposite her mother.* **Mrs Robinson** *has never seen her drink before. She never has drunk before.* **Elaine** *drinks her cocktail in two long drafts. Lights transform to evening.*

Scene Eight

Later. **Elaine** *and* **Mrs Robinson** *have been drinking.*

Mrs Robinson   'Laine.

Elaine   Don't want to.

Mrs Robinson   Go to bed.

Elaine   . . . no.

A pause.

Mom?

Mrs Robinson   Mm?

Elaine   'ove you.

Mrs Robinson   'ove you too.

Elaine   Huh!

Mrs Robinson   Oh yes.

Elaine   Don' believe you.

Mrs Robinson   In my *way*, OK? 'Laine . . .

Elaine   I don't be sick on my blouse.

Mrs Robinson   *Don't* be.

Elaine   No.

Mrs Robinson   Are you?

Elaine   No.

Mrs Robinson   Don't.

Elaine   No, I won't.

Mrs Robinson   I'm not apologise.

Elaine   Disgusting.

Mrs Robinson   I told you.

Elaine   Mmmng.

Mrs Robinson   . . . believe me?

Elaine   Mm.

Mrs Robinson   Gu.

Elaine *lurches over on to her hands and knees.*

Mrs Robinson   Not on the rug.

Elaine   Not going to.

Mrs Robinson   Get off the rug. Turn your head round.

Elaine *rolls on to her back. Begins to cry.*

Elaine   He sorrible. Everybody sorrible. Why so everybody horrible?

Mrs Robinson   My horrible?

Elaine   Yes.

Mrs Robinson   Mnot.

Elaine   Nnn. Nwhat are you then?

Mrs Robinson   Mbored. Sbored. N I din't anyway I tol' you. Was him.

Elaine   Hmph. Hm.

She sits up.

Be sick.

Mrs Robinson   Not my rug! . . . in your skirt!

Elaine   'S my favourite.

Mrs Robinson   'S horrible. Doesn't suit you.

Elaine   It's all right. It's all right. I don't want to.

Mrs Robinson   No fashion sense of dress. Never had.

Elaine   Rooms going over and over and over.

Mrs Robinson   It's . . . no, it's the little muscles. In your eyes. You got to relax a little muscles.

Elaine   Mmm?

Mrs Robinson   In the corner of your eyes. And let your eyes go up.

Elaine   Eragh . . . !

Mrs Robinson   Asright; they just want to drift up so just let 'em and they stay up there.

Elaine   Mmmhah.

Mrs Robinson   Relax and up they go an get stuck up there. Mmm?

Elaine   Oh yeh.

Mrs Robinson   And the room stops going over.

Elaine   Yeh.

Mrs Robinson   Mm?

Elaine   Mm.

Mrs Robinson   Little tip.

Elaine   'Kyou.

Mrs Robinson   Now just be still.

Elaine   Where's love go?

Mrs Robinson   Love?

Elaine Where's it all go?

Mrs Robinson   When you was little, I love you all the time.

Elaine   When I was little, yes, when I couldn't remember if you say so.

Mrs Robinson   I did.

Elaine   Well I don't remember and what about when I'm big? You love me? Look I'm big and you love me I don't think so.

Mrs Robinson   I do.

Elaine   You don't. Love gets littler and littler and goes away until it isn't there. It's all gone away.

Mrs Robinson   You love me?

Elaine   No. S'gone. You love daddy?

Mrs Robinson   No.

Elaine   See.

Mrs Robinson   That's long gone away somewhere I don't know.

Elaine So where's it go?

Mrs Robinson I met your father, he used t'sing t'me.
We'd be go someplace in the car and he used sing. He could
sing. He could. Same thing as Sinatra. Key. But not the
range. Not the high notes. I used to love him. Singing. In
the wee small hours. Just some songs he couldn't get to the
end. Couldn't get through those high notes to the end. You
know those notes. So. So. At school I'd had this teacher.
Who taught the choir. And the piano and oboe and things,
but the choir. So I know if you singing and you think you
breathing *in* as you go up . . . You understand? You imagine
you singing *in*, not up, not out, but *in*, then those high notes
can happen. La la la la . . .

Elaine La la la la la la . . .

Mrs Robinson La la . . . la la.

Elaine La la!

Mrs Robinson A's right. See? So. One night. In the car.
I taught him. I taught him how to do that. And right away,
he got it. How to do it. All the way. Half a thing. Octave.
(*She sings a snatch of Sinatra.*) And all the songs he used to sing
. . . to *want* to sing . . . suddenly he could. He could sing
them. And you know what? He never sang to me again.

Elaine I never heard him sing.

Mrs Robinson He'll never sing.

Elaine I'm going to have a forever love.

Mrs Robinson Ha.

Elaine No ha, never mind ha.

Mrs Robinson You never find it, sweetie.

Elaine I will.

Mrs Robinson You look hard as you like.

Elaine   You don't look. That's the thing. Everyone there's something.

Mrs Robinson   Something what?

Elaine   Worth loving.

Mrs Robinson   Hah.

Elaine   No, that's the point. You see? Don't *look*, that's not the point. The point . . . The *point* . . . You *choose*. You unnerstand?

Mrs Robinson   So young.

Elaine   The love's in *you*, and you just choose.

Mrs Robinson   Anyone 'cept Benjamin.

Elaine *laughs loudly.* **Mrs Robinson** *joins in. They laugh together.*

Mrs Robinson   'Xcept Benjamin.

Elaine   'Xcept Benjamin. *Anyone* except Benjamin.

Lights fade.

Scene Nine

The Braddocks' front lawn. **Mr Braddock** *is outside.* **Benjamin** *comes out the front door with a suitcase.*

Benjamin   Dad.

Dad   Mm?

Benjamin   Sir?

Dad   What?

Benjamin   I'm going to marry Elaine Robinson.

Dad   Are you serious?

Benjamin   Yes.

Dad   I'll go get your mother. You wait right here.

He leaves. **Benjamin** *puts on his jacket. His father comes back with his mother.*

Mom   What's all the excitement?

Dad   Ben.

Benjamin I'm going to marry Elaine Robinson.

Mom   Oh, Ben!

Dad   Ha hah!!!

Mom   Ah, Ben!

Dad   Ben and Elaine are getting married.

Mom   Oh Ben, I'm crying.

Mom *hugs him.*

Dad   Now let him go, let him go.

Mom *holds his hand.*

Dad   Let's get the whole story here. Have you set the date yet?

Benjamin   No.

Dad   Have you told the Robinsons yet?

Benjamin   No.

Dad   Let's call them right now.

Benjamin   No.

Mom   Oh, Ben.

Dad   Ben, we are . . . just delighted.

Benjamin   I think I should tell you that Elaine doesn't know about this yet.

Dad   She doesn't know about what yet?

Benjamin   That we're getting married.

Dad   What?

Benjamin   I just decided an hour ago.

Dad   And you talked it over with her?

Benjamin   No.

Dad   But you've written her about it?

Benjamin   No.

Dad   You called her?

Benjamin   No.

Dad   Well good God Ben, you get us all excited here and you haven't even proposed?

Benjamin   I'm driving up to Berkeley today.

Dad   To propose to her?

Benjamin   Yes.

Dad   Well that sounds kind of half-baked.

Benjamin   I'm moving up there.

Dad   To live?

Benjamin   Yes.

Mom   To *live*?

Dad   Now just a damn minute; she's up there finishing school and you're just going to move up there?

Benjamin   Yes.

Dad   Move up there and pester the girl because you have nothing better to do?

Benjamin   I love her.

Dad   You hardly know the girl, Ben; how do you know she wants to marry you?

Benjamin   Oh, she doesn't.

Dad   She what?

Benjamin   I'm pretty sure she won't want to initially.

Mom   Ben, does she like you?

Benjamin   No.

Dad/Mom   No?

Benjamin   She hates me.

Mom   Oh, Ben.

Blackout.

Act Two

Scene One

Attic room, Berkeley boarding house. Evening. **Benjamin** *stands holding the door open for* **Elaine**.

Elaine   Benjamin, why are you here?

Benjamin   Would you like to come in?

Elaine   I want to know what you're doing here in Berkeley.

Benjamin   Would you like some tea? I have tea.

Elaine   I want to know why you're stalking me.

Benjamin   I'm not.

Elaine   I see you on campus. You duck into doorways. On the bus you hid behind a magazine.

Benjamin   I've been meaning to speak to you.

Elaine   You've been following me around for days.

Benjamin   Would you like to come in?

Elaine   No.

Benjamin   Why not?

Elaine   I don't want to be in a room with you. Now why are you up here?

Benjamin   I'm just living here temporarily. I thought I might be bumping into you. I thought I remembered you were going to school up here.

Elaine   Did you move up here because of me?

Benjamin   No.

Elaine   Did you?

Benjamin   I don't know.

Elaine   Well, did you?

Benjamin   Well, what do you think?

Elaine   I think you did.

Benjamin   I'm just living in Berkeley. Having grown somewhat weary of family life. I've been meaning to stop by and pay my respects but have not been entirely certain how you felt about me after the incident with your mother which was certainly a serious mistake on my part but not serious enough I hope to permanently alter your feelings about me.

Elaine *comes in, slamming the door.*

Elaine   Benjamin, you are the one person in the world I never want to see again. I want you nowhere near me. I want you to leave here and never come back.

He holds his hands in front of his face.

Promise me you'll go.

Benjamin   Elaine . . .

Elaine   Promise me.

Benjamin (*stares at her a moment*)   All right.

Elaine   Pack you bags and go tonight.

Benjamin   All right!

Elaine   So promise me.

Benjamin   All right!

He flops down, his head in his arms.

Elaine   Goodbye, Benjamin.

Benjamin (*into his arms*)   I love you!!!!

Elaine   You what?

Benjamin   I love you! I love you and I can't help myself and I'm begging you to forgive me for what I did. I love you so much I'm terrified of seeing you every time I step outside the door I feel helpless and hopeless and lost and miserable, please forget what I did please Elaine oh God Elaine I love you please forget what I did Elaine I love you. I love you. Forget what I did. Please forget what I did Elaine, I love you.

Elaine   I don't think so.

Benjamin   I do.

Elaine   How can you love me Benjamin when you're so full of hate?

Benjamin   Of hate?

Elaine   How else could you have done that?

Benjamin   Done what?

Elaine   How could you have raped my mother?

Benjamin   What?

Elaine   You must have so much hate inside you.

Benjamin   Raped her?

Elaine *starts to cry.*

Benjamin   Did you say raped her?

Elaine   Virtually raped her.

Benjamin   Did she say that?

Elaine   I want you out of here by the morning.

Benjamin   No!

He runs between her and the door.

Elaine   Don't you touch me.

Benjamin   I'm not.

Elaine   Then get away from the door.

Benjamin   What did she say? Tell me what she said.

Elaine   Why?

Benjamin   Because it isn't true.

Elaine   She said you virtually raped her.

Benjamin   Which isn't true.

Elaine   Is it true you slept with her?

Benjamin   Yes.

Elaine   All right then, get away from the door.

Benjamin   What did she say?

Elaine   She said you dragged her up to the hotel room . . .

Benjamin   I dragged her!?

Elaine   . . . and you made her pass out and you raped her.

Benjamin   I what I drugged her?   I dragged her up five floors and I drugged her? I *raped* her?

Elaine   You *virtually*, yes.

Benjamin   I *what?*

Elaine   Could I leave now please?

Benjamin   That is not what happened.

Elaine   I have to leave.

Benjamin   My parents gave me a party when I got home from college. Your mother came up to my room.

Elaine   I don't want to hear this.

Benjamin   She asked me to unzip her dress.

Elaine   May I go now?

Benjamin   She took off all her clothes. She stood there entirely naked and she said . . .

Elaine *screams, long and hysterical.* **Benjamin** *frozen. She calms down. He brings her a chair. He brings her a glass of water. She drinks it.*

Elaine   What did you think would happen?

Benjamin   What?

Elaine   When you came up here?

Benjamin   I don't know.

He begins to pack.

Elaine   You just came up here?

Benjamin   I drove up. I made reservations at a restaurant.

Elaine   You were going to invite me to dinner?

Benjamin   Yes.

Elaine   Then what did you do?

Benjamin   I didn't invite you.

Elaine   I know.

Benjamin   I just came up here. I got this room. I kind of wallowed around. I wrote you some letters.

Elaine   Love letters?

Benjamin   I don't remember.

Elaine   So what are you going to do now?

Benjamin   I don't know.

Elaine   Where are you going?

Benjamin   I don't know.

Elaine   Well, what are you going to do?

Benjamin   Are you deaf?

Elaine   What?

Benjamin   I don't know what I'm going to do.

Elaine   Well, will you get on a bus or what?

Benjamin   Are you concerned about me or something?

Elaine   You came up here because of me. You messed up your life because of me, and now you're leaving because of me. You made me responsible! I don't want you drunk in some gutter because of me.

Benjamin   You want me to stick around?

Elaine   I want you to have a definite plan before you leave, then I want you to leave.

Benjamin   I have no plans.

Elaine   Then just make up your mind.

Benjamin   What?

Elaine   Don't you have a mind?

Benjamin   Of course.

Elaine   Then make it up.

Benjamin   I could go to Canada.

Elaine   You want to go to Canada?

Benjamin   No.

Elaine   You think I can study? You think I can think with you here?

Benjamin   Just tell me to leave and I'll leave.

Elaine   I have so much work this semester.

Benjamin   Would you just tell me to leave, please?

Elaine   Are you simple?

Benjamin What?

Elaine I mean what do I have to say to you?

Benjamin I don't know.

Elaine Can't you see the way I feel?

Benjamin Shall I go then?

Elaine Why don't you?

Benjamin Why don't I go?

Elaine Yes.

Benjamin All right. That's all you had to say.

Elaine *goes to the door.*

Elaine You know what she gave me for my eleventh birthday? She gave me a bartender's guide. I made her cocktails all day.

Benjamin She's a strange woman.

Elaine Is she attractive?

Benjamin Yes. Not really.

Elaine Well is she or not?

Benjamin I don't know.

Elaine You don't know which she is or you don't know which I'd like to hear?

Benjamin Either.

Elaine And am I?

Benjamin I'm sorry?

Elaine Am I as attractive as her?

Benjamin Oh, yes.

Elaine I have to go now.

Benjamin Would you marry me?

Elaine   Would I what?

Benjamin   Marry me. Would you?

Elaine   Marry you?

Benjamin   Yes.

Elaine Marry you?

Benjamin   Would you?

Elaine   Why would I?

Benjamin   I think we have a lot in common.

Elaine   Well, that's true.

Benjamin   So will you?

Elaine   Marry you?

Benjamin   Yes.

Elaine   Hah. Ha ha ha. Oh Benjamin, you are something.

Benjamin   Am I?

Elaine   Yes you are, but I don't know what. Why do you want to marry me?

Benjamin   It's the way I feel. I feel we should.

Elaine   What about the way I feel?

Benjamin   How do you feel?

Elaine   Confused.

Benjamin   Are you fond of me?

She sniffs.

Are you?

Elaine   Yes, fond.

Benjamin   Then let's get married.

Elaine   And can you imagine my parents?

Benjamin   You mean your mother?

Elaine   I mean my father.

Benjamin   I think he'd be very happy for us.

Elaine   And what if he found out what happened?

Benjamin   He won't.

Elaine   But what if he did?

Benjamin   I'd apologise. I'd say it was a stupid foolish thing and he'd say he was a little disappointed in me but if it's all in the past then that's that.

Elaine   You're so naïve.

Benjamin   Forget about your parents. This isn't about our parents. This is about us. Have you any other objections?

Elaine   Yes I do.

Benjamin   What are they?

Elaine   We're too young to be married. You should do other things first.

Benjamin   What other things?

Elaine   Well, *go* somewhere. Asia. Africa. See different places, different people.

Benjamin   Elaine, I have no desire to hop around the world ogling peasants. So do you have any other objections?

Elaine   Have you thought about finding a place to live and buying the groceries every day?

Benjamin   Sure.

Elaine   No you haven't.

Benjamin   You mean which brand of cereal we should buy?

Elaine   Yes.

Benjamin   No I haven't.

Elaine   Well why not? I mean that's the kind of thing you'll have to be thinking about, Benjamin, and I think you'd get sick of it after two days.

Benjamin   But I wouldn't get sick of you, would I?

Elaine   Well yes, I think you probably would.

Benjamin   Well no, I wouldn't.

Elaine   I'm not what you think I am, Benjamin. I'm just a plain ordinary person. I'm not smart or glamorous or anything like that.

Benjamin   So what?

Elaine   So why me?

Benjamin   Well. You're reasonably intelligent. You're striking-looking.

Elaine   Striking?

Benjamin   Sure.

Elaine   My ears are too prominent to be striking-looking.

Benjamin   No, they're very striking.

Elaine   I wouldn't be enough for you, Benjamin.

Benjamin   That isn't true.

Elaine   You're an intellectual, and I'm not.

Benjamin   Now listen . . .

Elaine   You should marry someone who can discuss politics and history and art . . .

Benjamin   Ah, shut up. Would you just . . . thank you. Now have you ever heard me talking about any of that crap?

Elaine   You majored in that crap.

Benjamin   Have you ever heard me talk about it?

Elaine   That crap?

Benjamin   Yes.

Elaine   No I haven't.

Benjamin   All right then. Goddammit, I hate all that. So will you marry me?

Elaine   No!

Benjamin   Why not?

Elaine   Well for a start I'm studying and you haven't got any money!

Benjamin   I'll move up here. I'll get a job teaching.

Elaine   I thought you didn't want to be a teacher.

Benjamin   Yes, but I could teach.

Elaine   You don't have the right attitude. Teachers are meant to be inspired.

Benjamin   That's a myth.

Elaine   Is it?

Benjamin   Oh yeh.

Elaine   It is not.

Benjamin   Any other objections?

Elaine   Plenty.

Benjamin   Take your best shot.

Elaine   Well, what about babies?

Benjamin   Babies?

Elaine   Do you want babies? Because that's what I want.

Benjamin   Well, I do too.

Elaine   Oh, come on.

Benjamin   I do.

Elaine   You do not.

Benjamin   Goddammit Elaine I want babies! Your babies. Triplets! I want to smother in a huge pile of diapers!

She laughs.

I'm serious here. Let's get married.

Elaine   Benjamin.

Benjamin   What?

Elaine   I can't see why I'm so attractive to you.

Benjamin   You just are.

Elaine   But . . . I don't understand.

Benjamin   What don't you understand?

Elaine   I mean you're a really brilliant person.

Benjamin   Elaine, don't start that. I mean it.

She nods. He takes her hand.

So, shall we get married?

Elaine   If you want to marry me so much why don't you just . . . drag me off.

Benjamin   All right, I will. We'll get a blood test in the morning and I'll just drag you off.

Elaine   But you can't. I mean I couldn't. I'd have to see Carl.

Benjamin   Carl?

Elaine   I'd have to talk to Carl first.

Benjamin   Who's Carl?

Elaine   The boy I met last semester. Carl Smith.

Benjamin   Well, what does he have to do with it?

Elaine   I said I might marry him.

Benjamin   What?

Elaine   He asked me to marry him and I said I might.

Benjamin   Well, Elaine . . .

Elaine   What?

Benjamin   Why in the hell didn't you tell me about this?

Elaine   I'm telling you.

Benjamin   Now? You're telling me now?

Elaine   Well there wasn't a before. It was none of your business before.

Benjamin   My God Elaine, how many people have done this?

Elaine   Proposed to me?

Benjamin   Yes.

Elaine   I don't know.

Benjamin   You mean more than him have?

Elaine   Well, yes.

Benjamin   How many?

Elaine   I don't know.

Benjamin   Well, could you try and remember? Six? Seven?

Elaine   About that, yes.

Benjamin   Are you kidding me?

Elaine   No.

Benjamin   You mean you have actually had six or seven people ask you to marry them?

Elaine   Is this any of your business?

Benjamin   Well yes, I think it is. When did he ask you?
Was it him on the bus?

Elaine   What bus?

Benjamin   On the bus to the zoo?

Elaine   You followed me to the zoo?

Benjamin   No, I missed the bus! When did he ask you?
Did he ask you that day? My God, he asked you that day,
didn't he? Where did he ask you, did he ask you at the zoo?

Elaine   Benjamin, why are you getting so excited?

Benjamin   He asked you at the zoo. I missed the bus and
he asked you in the monkey house or somewhere. Did he
get down on his knees? I hope he didn't get down on his
knees. He did, didn't he? What did he say?

Elaine   Benjamin . . .

Benjamin   What did he say?

Elaine   He said he thought we'd make a pretty good
team.

Benjamin   Hah!

Elaine   What?

Benjamin   He said that?

Elaine   Benjamin, what is wrong with you?

Benjamin   So what is he, a student?

Elaine   A medical student. Final year.

Benjamin   And he got down on his knees at the zoo and
he said . . .

Elaine   It wasn't at the zoo, it was at his apartment.

Benjamin   His apartment?

Elaine   Yes.

Benjamin   You went to his apartment?

Elaine   Yes.

Benjamin   But you . . . I mean you didn't . . . ?

Elaine   No, I did not spend the night.

Benjamin *grins.*

Benjamin   So good old Carl, the final-year medic, took you up to his apartment and popped the big one, did he . . . ?

Elaine   Goodbye Benjamin.

Benjamin   Did he put music on?

Elaine   I have to study.

Benjamin   No wait. Wait. Are we getting a blood test tomorrow?

Elaine   No.

Benjamin   The day after?

Elaine   I don't know.

Benjamin   Are we getting married?

Elaine   Maybe we are and maybe we aren't.

She leaves, closing the door behind her. **Benjamin** *sits. Suddenly the door opens,* **Elaine** *walks in, kisses him hard, and waltzes out again.* **Benjamin** *grins.*

Scene Two

The same. Morning. A knock on the door. **Benjamin** *opens it eagerly.* **Mr Robinson** *stands there. He's been travelling all night. He's dishevelled.*

Mr Robinson   Do you want . . . Do you want to try and tell me why you did it?

Benjamin I don't . . . I don't . . .

Mr Robinson *comes in and sits down.*

Mr Robinson Do you have any special grudge against me you'd like to tell me about? Do you feel a particularly strong resentment for me for some reason?

Benjamin No. It's not . . .

Mr Robinson Is there something I've said that's caused this contempt? Or is it just the things I stand for that you despise?

Benjamin It was nothing to do with you, sir.

Mr Robinson Well Ben, it was quite a bit to do with me. And I'd like to hear your feelings about me if you have any. I'd like to know why you've done this to me.

Benjamin There was no personal . . . It was nothing personal.

Mr Robinson Nothing personal?

Benjamin No, sir.

Mr Robinson Well that's an interesting way of looking at it, Ben. You sleep with another man's wife . . .

Benjamin Mr Robinson, there was no reason for it . . .

Mr Robinson Ben, you're a little old to abdicate responsibility . . .

Benjamin I'm entirely responsible. It was altogether my own fault, Mr Robinson, but I would like you to know that . . .

Mr Robinson I think we're two civilised human beings; do you think it's necessary to threaten each other?

Benjamin No I don't.

Mr Robinson Then do you want to unclench your fists please? Thank you.

Benjamin   I'm trying to tell you that I have no personal feelings about you, Mr Robinson. I'm trying to tell you I do not resent you.

Mr Robinson   You don't respect me terribly much either, do you?

Benjamin   No, I don't.

Mr Robinson *nods*.

Mr Robinson   Well, I don't think we have a whole lot to say to each other, Ben. I do think you should know the consequences of what you've done. I do think you should know my wife and I are getting a divorce.

Benjamin   A divorce? Why?

Mr Robinson   Why?

Benjamin   Well, it shouldn't make *that* much difference, surely? I mean we . . . we . . . got into bed with each other but it was nothing compared to . . . It was nothing at all. We could have been shaking hands.

Mr Robinson   I always thought when you took your clothes off and got into bed with a woman and had sexual intercourse with her that was just a little more than shaking hands.

Benjamin   Not in this case.

Mr Robinson   Well, that's not saying much for my wife, is it?

Benjamin   You miss the point.

Mr Robinson   Not at all Ben. I'm sure my wife's bedroom technique could do with a little brushing up.

Benjamin   You are distorting everything I say!

Mr Robinson   Don't shout at me, Ben.

Benjamin   The point is I don't love your wife; I love your daughter.

Mr Robinson   Well, I'm sure you think you do Ben, but after a few times shaking hands with Elaine I'm sure you'll find her just as disappointing.

Benjamin   I'm sorry?

Mr Robinson   A boy called us up and he asked for her hand. Carl is to be a doctor, and he asked for her hand in marriage. There are some fine young men in this world.

Benjamin   Mr Robinson . . .

Mr Robinson   I don't know if I can prosecute or not, but I think maybe I can. In light of what's happened I think maybe I can get you behind bars if you even so much as look at my daughter again. I don't want to mince words with you. I think you're totally despicable. I think you're scum. I think you're filth.

He leaves. Enter **Dad**.

Benjamin   Dad?

Dad   I have just driven a grown man four hundred miles, Ben. A grown man crying like a child because of what you did to him. He was sobbing, Ben, beating his hand on the armrest like a little baby. Now pack your case.

Benjamin   I can't leave here.

Dad   You're driving back with me tonight.

Benjamin   I appreciate your concern but I can't leave here.

Dad   Hal's going to spend a couple of days with his daughter. And you have an appointment in the morning with a psychiatrist.

Benjamin   I beg your pardon?

Dad   Get to it, Ben.

Benjamin   Well, I don't know if you brought a straitjacket up here with you, but if you didn't . . .

Dad *hits his son very hard with the back of his hand.* **Benjamin** *goes flying.*

Dad Forgive me for that, Ben. I'm very badly shaken. I want you to forgive me for that.

Blackout.

Scene Three

A psychiatrist's study.

The **Psychiatrist** *with his back to us.* **Benjamin**, **Dad** *and* **Mom** *in chairs facing us.* **Mom** *is nearly hysterical.*

Mom Well, I just don't understand what I'm supposed to have done! Why is it all my fault?

Dad Now, that's not what he said.

Mom He said it was my fault.

Dad He didn't say that.

Benjamin It certainly sounded like that.

Dad You keep your goddam opinions to yourself!

Mom Why is everything *my* fault?

Dad Would you . . . Would you please . . . Could you just, for the love of Mike . . . *say* something?

A pause.

Psychiatrist Nothing is anyone's fault.

Benjamin Well, that's encouraging.

Mom I don't understand if you do your very best and you're a perfectly decent person how you can be blamed for things you didn't do even if the person who did them you once, you what, you didn't take him to the zoo or something or he didn't like green beans? I cooked three vegetables half my whole life, I stood in line for a plastic man with the right

sort of gun in a *blizzard* for Heaven's sake, all Christmas
Eve . . .

Dad   Would you just shut up for thirty seconds!

Mom   I just want to know . . .

Dad   Well then, *listen* for once in your life!

A pause.

Doctor . . .

Psychiatrist   I'm not a doctor.

Dad   You're not?

Psychiatrist   But that's OK.

Dad   Well whatever you are, I don't know what we're all
doing here but the situation's very simple. Our son – I still
like to call him our son – has behaved so reprehensibly
towards the wife and daughter of my oldest and dearest
friend there is obviously something not entirely normal . . .

Benjamin   Define normal.

Dad   I'm speaking, Benjamin.

Benjamin   You try and put your own son in a hospital
with old women muttering obscenities and and murderers
peeing in the corridor. Is that normal?

Mom   It's for your own good, Benjamin.

Benjamin   And they've hidden her. Did you know that?
The Robinsons kidnapped their own daughter and took her
to New England. Is that normal?

Dad   That's just until the wedding.

Benjamin   The what?

Dad   The whatever.

Benjamin   What wedding?

A pause.

What wedding?

Mom   I'm not saying I'm entirely blameless . . .

Benjamin   Am I insane?

Dad   It's all for the best, Ben.

Benjamin   Excuse me, I asked you a question, am I insane?

Psychiatrist   I don't believe so.

Benjamin   Thank you.

Benjamin *jumps out the window.*

Dad   Benjamin!

Mom   Benjamin!

Dad   You come back here!

Mom (*losing control*)   Oh God, it's all my fault!

Scene Four

The vestry, First Presbyterian church. Door to the body of the church, door a large cupboard.

Solemn organ music, then the sound of a row rapidly rising until **Benjamin** *bursts in pulling* **Elaine** *by the wrist.* **Elaine** *is in full white wedding gown. He slams the door behind them and runs to the other door.*

Elaine   Benjamin!

Benjamin   It's OK Elaine, everything's going to be OK now.

Elaine   What are you doing? Benjamin!

He flings open the other door and an old pew falls out on him.

Benjamin   Oh God.

Elaine What are we doing?

Benjamin We went the wrong way.

Mr Robinson (*off*)   YOU SON OF A BITCH!

Mrs Robinson *runs in just before* **Benjamin** *slams the door and uses the old pew to barricade it. Immediately,* **Mr Robinson**'*s weight hits the door from the other side.*

Mrs Robinson   Elaine!

Mr Robinson (*off*)   Let me in there you filthy degenerate!

Others shout and holler on the other side of the door. **Mrs Robinson** *stands getting her breath back, staring at* **Benjamin**. **Benjamin** *gets his breath back staring at* **Mrs Robinson**.

Mrs Robinson   Elaine, get back in the church.

Elaine   Benjamin, what is happening?

Benjamin   We're getting married.

Elaine   I'm getting married to Carl.

Benjamin   You're going to marry me.

Elaine   I'm marrying Carl. I was just marrying him.

Mr Robinson (*off*)   Open this door, you filthy, degenerate son of bitch!

Elaine   You hit my fiancé!

Benjamin   He fainted.

Elaine   Well, you bloodied his nose.

Mr Robinson (*off*)   Judith, open the door!

Mrs Robinson   Open the door, Benjamin.

Benjamin   No.

Mrs Robinson   Open the door.

Benjamin   You think I'm mad?

Mrs Robinson   Like a dog. You should be shot.

Benjamin   I love Elaine. Elaine, I love you.

Mr Robinson (*off*)   I'm calling the police, you pervert.

Mrs Robinson   So this is, what is this, Benjamin? A big romantic gesture?

Benjamin   I just want to get married.

Mrs Robinson   So does Elaine.

Benjamin   Not to him.

Mrs Robinson   She wants to get married to Carl.

Benjamin   No she doesn't.

Mrs Robinson   Yes she does.

Benjamin   Elaine, do you want to marry Carl?

Elaine   Yes, I do.

Benjamin   No she doesn't.

Mrs Robinson   Do you want to marry Carl, Elaine?

Elaine   Yes I do.

Benjamin   No you don't.

Mrs Robinson   I think she does Benjamin.

Benjamin   You don't have to do this Elaine. You don't have to do everything your mother says.

Mr Robinson (*off*)   You're a dead man, Braddock.

Benjamin   Do you love me?

Mrs Robinson   Love?

Benjamin   Elaine, do you love me?

Elaine   No.

Benjamin   Well, I think you do.

Mrs Robinson   She doesn't love you, Benjamin.

Benjamin   Yes she does.

Elaine   I don't.

Benjamin   You see?

Mr Robinson (*off*)   This is kidnap, Braddock. You could do life for this! You could go to the chair for this!

Mrs Robinson   I don't know what you think you're going to achieve here.

Benjamin   Well that's because you have a very limited imagination.

Mrs Robinson   All that's going to happen is you're going to be seriously assaulted and Elaine is going to marry Carl.

Benjamin   I don't think so.

Mrs Robinson   Elaine, will you please put this poor boy out of his misery? Will you please tell him he's making a complete ass of himself.

Benjamin   Would you tell your mother that you love me? Would you please do that?

Elaine   Would you please both stop telling me what I think!

Benjamin   So why are you marrying Carl?

Elaine   I don't have to tell you that.

Benjamin   Because your parents told you to.

Elaine   Do you think so little of me?

Benjamin   Then why are you marrying him?

Elaine   Carl is a perfectly decent man.

Benjamin   Perfectly decent?

Elaine   I think that's a lot.

Benjamin   I think you'll make a great team.

Elaine   Well, thank you.

Benjamin   But is that enough?

Elaine   Of course that's not enough!

Benjamin   Then why are you marrying Carl?

Elaine   Because I am.

Benjamin   Is that a reason?

Elaine   Yes it is.

Benjamin   No it isn't, it's an evasion.

Elaine   Well, it's a fact, Benjamin.

Benjamin   Why is it?

Elaine   Why is it what?

Benjamin   Why are you marrying Carl?

Elaine   You know why.

Benjamin   No I don't.

Elaine   I think you do.

Benjamin   Then tell me why you're marrying him!!

Elaine   Because if I don't marry Carl you are going to ruin my life.

Benjamin   How?

Mrs Robinson   Being in it, Benjamin.

Benjamin   You're marrying Carl because you love me.

Elaine   Benjamin, that is . . .

Mrs Robinson   Absurd.

Benjamin   But it's true. Say it's not true.

Mrs Robinson   Say it's not true, Elaine.

Elaine   It's not.

Benjamin   Say it's not.

Elaine   I just said.

Benjamin   You love me. I know it.

Mrs Robinson   Keep quiet, Elaine.

Elaine   If I marry you my life is ruined.

Benjamin   No it isn't.

Mrs Robinson   Yes it is.

Benjamin   It wouldn't be.

Mrs Robinson   Believe me, both of you, it would.

Benjamin   You know something Mrs Robinson, you are a bitch. I mean I'm sorry to be rude but you are a one-hundred-carat solid gold bitch. Elaine, take off that dress.

Elaine   My dress?

Benjamin   You're not getting married. Take off the dress.

Mrs Robinson   Benjamin you are digging a very deep hole for yourself.

Benjamin   I'm sure you'd like to think so.

Mrs Robinson   Immoral behaviour, kidnapping, sexual assault . . .

Benjamin   All I want is to marry Elaine.

Mrs Robinson   He's not what you think he is Elaine. He's not the sensitive soul you think. He's got a selfish streak so wide it hides his vicious streak. What he doesn't disdain he despises. And that includes himself. He's lazy, self-loathing, and not much fun to be with. And he's terrible in bed.

Benjamin   No I'm not.

Mrs Robinson   Yes you are.

Benjamin   Oh no I'm not.

Mrs Robinson   Oh but yes you are.

Benjamin   Am I?

Mrs Robinson   Oh yes.

Benjamin   Am I?

Mrs Robinson   Yes.

Benjamin   Am I?

Mrs Robinson (*faltering*)   Yes you are. He is.

Benjamin   I love you Elaine. Take off the dress.

Elaine   Benjamin, I . . .

Benjamin   Will you TAKE OFF THAT GODDAM DRESS!

He pulls down the zip and tugs it off her shoulders.

Elaine   Ow! Benjamin!!!

Mr Robinson *starts hitting the door with a fire axe.*

Benjamin   Jesus.

Mr Robinson   You lowlife scum!

Mrs Robinson   Oh my God.

Mr Robinson   You excremental piece of garbage!

Another blow.

Benjamin   Mr Robinson . . .

Mr Robinson   You depraved son of a bitch!!!

Another blow and a panel crashes out. An arm through the hole to dislodge the bench and he's in, slamming what's left of the door behind him. **Wedding Guests** *peer in.*

Benjamin   Mr Robinson, I can understand you feeling quite upset . . .

Mr Robinson   I'm going to cut your sick head off.

Elaine   Daddy, don't.

Guests (*variously*)   Calm down, Howard./He ain't worth it, Howard./Attaboy, Howard./Frank, you shush now.

Elaine   Daddy, please.

Mr Robinson   It's all right, Peaches. I'm in control here.

Mrs Robinson   Take it easy, Howard.

Mr Robinson   Everything's under control.

The **Priest** *pushes his way to the front of the throng and examines his vestry door.*

Mrs Robinson   Put the axe down, Howard.

Priest   Mr Robinson . . .

Mr Robinson   It's all right, Reverend. I'm in control. I'm in control.

Elaine   Daddy, put it down.

Mr Robinson   You seduce my wife, you harass my daughter, you abduct her, you attempt to undress her in a holy place . . .

Mrs Robinson   Howard, put the axe down.

Mr Robinson   You said I should kill him. As we ran down the aisle you said: 'Kill him, Howard.'

Mrs Robinson   I changed my mind.

Benjamin   That's very generous of you.

Mrs Robinson   Shut up, Benjamin.

Elaine   Daddy, put the axe down. I'm marrying Carl. Nothing's going to change. Everything's OK. A door got damaged. I'm marrying Carl.

Mr Robinson *drops the axe. Slumps.*

Mr Robinson   Are you OK?

Mrs Robinson   I need a drink.

Elaine   I'm fine.

Mr Robinson *looks round at the door. Goes to the* **Priest**. *Pulls out his wallet.*

Mr Robinson   Um . . . I don't have anything on me. Reverend, would you do me the courtesy of sending me an invoice for the door?

Elaine   Everybody please go back? We'll be out with you soon.

The **Priest** *ushers the throng away.*

Priest   Could we all please move back into the body of the church? Is the groom conscious?

Elaine *tends to her father.*

Elaine   You have some varnish in your hair.

Mr Robinson   I'm fine.

Elaine   Are you OK?

Mr Robinson   Uh-huh.

Elaine   Ready to give me away?

Benjamin   Elaine . . .

Elaine   I don't want to go against the world, Benjamin. I know you hate your parents, and my parents. I know you hate everybody's parents and I know you want to go against the world but I don't want that.

Benjamin *sits, his head in his hands.*

Elaine   Daddy.

Mr Robinson   Yes.

Elaine *takes his arm and leads him out. A murmur of consent from the congregation beyond.*

Mrs Robinson   You know what? You never stood a chance. She never made a decision in her life without climbing into her father's lap for a couple of hours.

Benjamin   It's not what she wants.

Mrs Robinson   When Elaine was two years old and all the other brats were screaming, she sat and read picture books.

Unseen by **Mrs Robinson**, **Elaine** *returns for her corsage.*

When she was seven she never asked for a Tootsie Roll, let alone Disneyland. All through her teens she never came home late, drunk, her blouse unbuttoned or her ears pierced. Elaine's never *wanted* anything.

Benjamin   Is that so?

Mrs Robinson   I've waited twenty years to see if she developed any personality of her own but no, she's ten per cent me and ninety per cent him. I'm the curiosity, and the eye. He's the dreary diligence and the enduring dullness. Beyond that, Benjamin, there *is* no Elaine.

Elaine   Is that what you think?

Mrs Robinson *turns and is speechless.*

Benjamin   I don't think that, Elaine.

Elaine   That I'm what, that I'm . . .

Benjamin   I think you're a wonderful person.

Mrs Robinson   Elaine . . .

Elaine   Is that what you *think*?

Mrs Robinson   Why should you care what I think? Why should you care what anyone thinks?

Elaine   You think I'm nothing?

Mrs Robinson   I never said that.

Benjamin   That's exactly what she said.

Elaine   That I only do what I'm told?

Mrs Robinson   You're a wonderful girl.

Elaine   If I don't do what I'm told you scream at me.

Mrs Robinson   Elaine . . .

Elaine   You throw my dolls out the window, you tear my posters from the wall, you humiliate me in front of a perfectly nice boy and it's my senior prom!

Mrs Robinson   Well then scream back, Elaine. Cover your wall in weeping kittens. Go to your prom looking like a birthday cake. Ignore your mother, the unfeeling bitch, and do what you damn well want to!

Elaine   Go to the clinic and get rid of the baby?

Benjamin   I'm sorry?

Elaine   I said 'Go to the clinic and get rid of the baby.'

Mrs Robinson   Are you pregnant?

Elaine   No, I'm not. You were. So why didn't you do what you damn well wanted to?

Elaine *starts to cry.* **Mrs Robinson** *can't bring herself to step forward and comfort her.* **Benjamin** *does,* **Elaine** *clings to* **Benjamin**. **Mr Robinson** *returns.*

Mr Robinson   Elaine? What in God's name is going on?

Mrs Robinson   Leave them alone, Howard.

Mr Robinson   What?

Mrs Robinson   See to the guests.

Mr Robinson   Are you condoning this . . . this . . . what is this?

Benjamin   May I say something?

Mrs Robinson   No. Howard would you please go and announce to the guests that the wedding is cancelled.

Mr Robinson   You *are* condoning this. What the hell is this? Peaches . . .

Elaine   Leave me alone. Would you both just leave me alone. Leave us alone.

Mr Robinson   I don't understand.

Mrs Robinson   I think Peaches is rebelling, Howard.

Mr Robinson   Elaine?

Elaine   I'm sorry.

Mr Robinson   Are you going to let her *do* this? Am I the only one left in this family with a shred of decency?

Mrs Robinson   Relax Howard, give us a song.

Mr Robinson   A what?

Mrs Robinson   Sing me a song. Or speak to my attorney.

Mr Robinson (*quietly*)   Braddock, one dark night. . .

Mrs Robinson   You don't have to kill him Howard. Leave them alone and they'll *bore* one another to death.

Mr Robinson   This wedding cost five thousand dollars.

Mrs Robinson   Then for Christ's sake let's go get a *drink*.

She moves him out the door.

Elaine   Mom . . .

Mrs Robinson   It's a little late for affection Elaine. This was my sole gesture of support. Marry this conniving son of a bitch and you're on your own.

Elaine   The hell with you.

Mrs Robinson   Bless.

Elaine *swings round and kisses* **Benjamin**. *They are isolated for a few moments in their embrace before a seedy motel manager unlocks a door and they find themselves alone in . . .*

Scene Five

A motel room somewhere in Nevada. Headlights sweep through the blinds. **Benjamin** *and* **Elaine** *look around them.*

Benjamin   It's a dump.

Elaine   It's a room. It's cute. It's one o'clock in the morning.

She takes off the raincoat and stands in her wedding dress.

Well, I guess we did it. I guess we ought to get blood tests. If we want children. I mean if we want them I guess it'd be best they were normal. What are you thinking?

Benjamin   What sort of cereal.

Elaine   Huh?

Benjamin   What sort of cereal?

Elaine   Oh.

She smiles.

Cheerios.

Benjamin   Cheerios.

Elaine   OK?

Benjamin   OK.

Benjamin *puts down suitcase and is about to open it.*

Elaine   Would you undo my dress?

He does. She's shy, but continues undressing. **Benjamin** *doesn't move.*

Could I have a cigarette?

Benjamin *lights her a cigarette. She smokes like her mother. She finishes undressing and lies on the bed.* **Benjamin** *doesn't move.*

Elaine   Benjamin?

She loses confidence and covers herself.

Maybe you're right.

Benjamin *just stands there.*

Elaine   Maybe we should wait.

Benjamin *doesn't speak.*

Elaine   Maybe I should graduate.

Benjamin *can't think of a thing to say.*

Elaine   I mean, you don't have the first idea of what to do with me, do you?

Benjamin *opens his suitcase and looks at her over the lid. Then he brings out a pack of Cheerios. She laughs with delight.*

Elaine   How did you know that?

Elaine *opens the Cheerios.*

Benjamin   I'll go to the front desk. They may have some milk.

Elaine   No. Don't go. There never was any milk. I like 'em rocky.

He sits on the bed and eats a handful.

Don't just wolf them, Benjamin. You have to sort them out first. Oatmeal. Wheatmeal. Rice. OK?

Benjamin   OK.

Elaine   Improves the flavour.

Benjamin   Yes, it does.

They sit on the bed and eat Cheerios.

End.

Methuen Modern Plays
include work by

Jean Anouilh
John Arden
Margaretta D'Arcy
Peter Barnes
Sebastian Barry
Brendan Behan
Dermot Bolger
Edward Bond
Bertolt Brecht
Howard Brenton
Anthony Burgess
Simon Burke
Jim Cartwright
Caryl Churchill
Noël Coward
Lucinda Coxon
Sarah Daniels
Nick Darke
Nick Dear
Shelagh Delaney
David Edgar
David Eldridge
Dario Fo
Michael Frayn
John Godber
Paul Godfrey
David Greig
John Guare
Peter Handke
David Harrower
Jonathan Harvey
Iain Heggie
Declan Hughes
Terry Johnson
Sarah Kane
Charlotte Keatley
Barrie Keeffe
Howard Korder

Robert Lepage
Stephen Lowe
Doug Lucie
Martin McDonagh
John McGrath
Terrence McNally
David Mamet
Patrick Marber
Arthur Miller
Mtwa, Ngema & Simon
Tom Murphy
Phyllis Nagy
Peter Nichols
Joseph O'Connor
Joe Orton
Louise Page
Joe Penhall
Luigi Pirandello
Stephen Poliakoff
Franca Rame
Mark Ravenhill
Philip Ridley
Reginald Rose
David Rudkin
Willy Russell
Jean-Paul Sartre
Sam Shepard
Wole Soyinka
Shelagh Stephenson
C. P. Taylor
Theatre de Complicite
Theatre Workshop
Sue Townsend
Judy Upton
Timberlake Wertenbaker
Roy Williams
Victoria Wood

Methuen Contemporary Dramatists
include

Peter Barnes (three volumes)
Sebastian Barry
Edward Bond (six volumes)
Howard Brenton
  (two volumes)
Richard Cameron
Jim Cartwright
Caryl Churchill (two volumes)
Sarah Daniels (two volumes)
Nick Darke
David Edgar (three volumes)
Ben Elton
Dario Fo (two volumes)
Michael Frayn (two volumes)
Paul Godfrey
John Guare
Peter Handke
Jonathan Harvey
Declan Hughes
Terry Johnson (two volumes)
Bernard-Marie Koltès
David Lan
Bryony Lavery
Doug Lucie
David Mamet (three volumes)

Martin McDonagh
Duncan McLean
Anthony Minghella
  (two volumes)
Tom Murphy (four volumes)
Phyllis Nagy
Anthony Nielsen
Philip Osment
Louise Page
Joe Penhall
Stephen Poliakoff
  (three volumes)
Christina Reid
Philip Ridley
Willy Russell
Ntozake Shange
Sam Shepard (two volumes)
Wole Soyinka (two volumes)
David Storey (three volumes)
Sue Townsend
Michel Vinaver (two volumes)
Michael Wilcox
David Wood (two volumes)
Victoria Wood

Methuen World Classics
include

Jean Anouilh (two volumes)
John Arden (two volumes)
Arden & D'Arcy
Brendan Behan
Aphra Behn
Bertolt Brecht (six volumes)
Büchner
Bulgakov
Calderón
Čapek
Anton Chekhov
Noël Coward (seven volumes)
Eduardo De Filippo
Max Frisch
John Galsworthy
Gogol
Gorky
Harley Granville Barker
  (two volumes)
Henrik Ibsen (six volumes)
Lorca (three volumes)

Marivaux
Mustapha Matura
David Mercer (two volumes)
Arthur Miller (five volumes)
Molière
Musset
Peter Nichols (two volumes)
Clifford Odets
Joe Orton
A. W. Pinero
Luigi Pirandello
Terence Rattigan
  (two volumes)
W. Somerset Maugham
  (two volumes)
August Strindberg
  (three volumes)
J. M. Synge
Ramón del Valle-Inclán
Frank Wedekind
Oscar Wilde